pasta

Life is a combination of magic and pasta.
Federico Fellini

Pasta

POCKETBOOK

Rose Elliot

Little Books by Big Names™

First published in the United Kingdom in 2004 by Little Books Ltd,
48 Catherine Place, London SW1E 6HL

10 9 8 7 6 5 4 3 2 1

A CIP catalogue record for this book is available from the British Library.
Some of the recipes in this book previously appeared in *Rose Elliot's
Vegetarian Pasta*, HarperCollinsPublishers 1997/HarperCollinsIllustrated 1999.

ISBN: 1 904435 19 X

Many thanks to: Jamie Ambrose for editorial production and management,
Claudia Dowell for proofreading, Two Associates for jacket design,
Mousemat Design for layout design, Craig Campbell of QSP Print
for printing consultancy. Printed and bound in Scotland by Scotprint.

contents

pasta basics

Who doesn't love pasta? Cheap to buy, convenient to store, quick and easy to use, tasty and satisfying to eat, it's the perfect any-time meal. It's also blissfully reliable, and there are always some new and easy ideas for using it.

For all these reasons, I decided to gather what I consider to be my one hundred all-time best pasta recipes and put them together in this handy pocketbook. Here, you'll find many different types of delicious pasta dishes in one neat, convenient book, which, because of its handy size, doubles as a supermarket shopping list. Instead of writing down your ingredients, simply take the *Pasta Pocketbook* with you when shopping to avoid forgetting any crucial items.

shapes
Pasta comes in an almost endless variety of shapes and sizes. While experts are very fussy about what shape they put with which sauce, you should really choose whatever combination you like.

That said, the classic combinations developed for a reason, and they can be useful as guidelines. Long, slippery pastas such as spaghetti (my all-time favourite), go best with smooth sauces which will cling to them, like tomato. Short pastas marry well with chunkier sauces, although long pasta with coils and frilly bits work well with heartier sauces, too, because the vegetable chunks get caught in the curls.

Ribbon pastas, such as tagliatelle, fettucine and pappardelle, are more delicate – just made for creamy sauces – although pappardelle, another of my favourites, with its big, thick ribbons, is nicely complemented by strong flavours such as wild mushrooms, fresh basil and tasty Parmesan.

The short tubes, such as penne and rigatone, are the most adaptable. These are the best 'all-rounders', good with lots of different sauces, which they trap in their cavities, making the sauce easy to eat; they're also excellent with chunky ingredients. I'm particularly fond of penne rigate.

Special shapes such as conchiglie (shells), fusilli (spirals), farfalle (butterflies or bow ties) and lumache (snails) are also perfect for mixing with chunky ingredients and are great in pasta salads. Remember that the pasta called gnocchi is named after the small potato dumpling whose shape it copies. If you simply ask for 'gnocchi', you may get potato dumplings instead, so always request the pasta version.

Soup pastas are tiny and include many pretty shapes such as stelline (little stars), farfalline (baby butterflies), alfabetini (little letters of the alphabet), and orzi, which look like grains of rice.

There are literally hundreds of different pasta shapes. For the purposes of this book, however, I've used pasta shapes that are easy to find, either in supermarkets or Italian shops.

As well as the Italian pastas, there are also oriental noodles. I have included a couple of recipes using these, concentrating on the ones that are widely available. They are prepared differently from Italian pasta, requiring only a soaking in boiling water before use. Like Italian pasta, they can quickly turn a stir-fry or soup into a more substantial dish.

Some oriental pastas are made from grains other than wheat: rice and buckwheat, for instance. These are delicious, and particularly useful for people who want or need to avoid wheat in their diet. You can also get special wheat-free pastas from supermarkets and health-food shops; some taste very like the real thing. In my experience they need careful cooking, however, because they quickly lose their *al dente* quality.

On the subject of different pastas, many shapes can be found in a wholemeal variety, mostly from health shops, though many supermarkets today do stock some. You either love them or loathe them. They have a nutty flavour and they do contain more fibre, which makes a normal diet healthier. But lentil, bean and vegetable sauces can also be useful sources of fibre.

fresh or dried?

People always ask whether it is worth buying fresh pasta. Well, the Italians I know prefer the dried type. If you were able to get it freshly made by a top chef, I'm sure fresh pasta would be divine. But most widely available fresh pasta is disappointingly heavy.

Stuffed pastas like ravioli, tortellini and cappelletti are an exception to this rule – they're meant to be bought fresh – but you do need to be selective. Some can be very heavy, while perfectly made ones melt in your mouth. I haven't included recipes using these, because all you need to do is to cook them and serve with butter or olive oil, a few chopped herbs, perhaps, or at most, a light cream or tomato sauce, for which there are recipes in this book.

flavoured pastas

You can spend quite a lot of money on flavoured pastas and I find these entrancing to look at – lovely pink beetroot pasta, red tomato pasta, green spinach pasta, golden saffron pasta – but that's where the love affair ends. Apart from the occasional use of spinach pasta at the right time and place, I really don't like flavoured pastas. For me, coloured pastas belong in a pretty glass jar where I can enjoy the look of them. But feel free to disagree.

cooking pasta

A good rule of thumb is to allow 100–125g (3½–4oz) pasta per person, 1–1.2 litres (1¾–2 pints) water and ¼ teaspoon of salt per every 100g of pasta. Use a large saucepan so that the pasta can move around as it cooks. First bring the saucepan of water to the boil, then add the pasta. Some experts also throw in the salt at this time, and they swear that it affects the cooking, texture and so on. Personally, I prefer to cook pasta without salt in the water and add salt to taste after draining.

When you've put the pasta in, cover the pan with the lid briefly to bring it quickly back to the boil. Once this happens, remove the lid and let the pasta continue at a rolling boil until it's *al dente* – just tender but with a firm bite. This may take less time than stated on the packet, so start testing in good time by lifting out a piece of pasta and biting it. In the recipes in this book I've mostly given an average time of eight minutes, but always use your own judgement and always test the pasta after the first few minutes.

When the pasta is done, tip it into a colander and shake it gently to remove excess water. You don't need to get the pasta dry; indeed, it's better to leave some water still clinging to it. Then you can either put the pasta into a large warmed bowl with some olive oil and any other ingredients you are using, or tip it back into the still-warm saucepan before adding the oil and other additions and tossing well. Finally, you can either serve it out and top with the sauce, or if you prefer, add the sauce to the pasta in the pan or bowl and mix before serving. Eat immediately – and *buon appetito!*

pasta sauces

Just as there are basic pasta shapes from which to build a whole host of recipes, five basic sauces (also known as the 'classic sauces', but don't let that frighten you) can be used to create a wide variety of dishes. Three of them – béchamel, lentil bolognese, and tomato – also freeze exceptionally well, so it can be helpful to make double the amount of these and put one batch away for a rainy day. Pesto and cream sauces keep well, tightly covered, in the refrigerator; you can store pesto for up to two weeks this way, and cream for a couple of days.

Just like the rest of the recipes in this book, all of the sauce recipes have been designed to serve four, unless otherwise specified.

basic cream sauce

25g or 1oz butter

1 onion, peeled and chopped

2 garlic cloves, peeled and crushed

300ml or 10fl oz cream: single, double or soya

salt and freshly ground pepper

freshly grated nutmeg

1 Melt the butter in a small saucepan, then add the onion. Cover and cook gently for ten minutes, until tender, not brown.

2 Add the garlic and cook a minute or so longer. Stir in the cream and leave to simmer gently for about ten minutes, until the cream has reduced and thickened.

3 Season with salt, pepper and nutmeg, and keep to one side until the pasta is done.

basic béchamel sauce

55g or 2oz butter

40g or 1½oz flour

600ml or 20fl oz milk

1 bay leaf

a few stalks of parsley, if available

slice of onion, if available

a little extra milk (see method)

4–8 tablespoons cream, optional

salt and freshly ground pepper

freshly grated nutmeg

1 Melt the butter in a small saucepan and stir in the flour. When it froths, stir in half the milk and beat well over the heat until it thickens. Add the rest of the milk and keep stirring vigorously, still over the heat, until the sauce is thick and smooth.

2 Add the bay leaf, parsley stalks and slice of onion (if using), then leave the sauce over a very low heat for ten minutes. Thin the sauce by stirring in a little extra milk if necessary. If making the sauce well in advance, do not stir in this extra milk, but pour it over the top of the sauce and leave it to prevent a skin forming.

3 When ready to use, give the sauce a stir, remove the bay leaf, parsley and onion, add the cream (if you're using it) and season with salt, pepper and nutmeg.

basic pesto sauce

55g or 2oz fresh basil leaves

2 garlic cloves, peeled

2 tablespoons pine nuts, toasted

8 tablespoons olive oil

55g or 2oz freshly grated Parmesan cheese, optional

salt and freshly ground pepper

squeeze of lemon juice, optional

1 Put the basil leaves, garlic gloves and pine nuts into a food processor or blender, with a little of the olive oil. Whizz to a fairly smooth paste.

2 Gradually, add the rest of the oil, whizzing as you go, then transfer the mixture to a bowl, or to a screwtop jar if you're planning to keep the pesto in the fridge. Stir in the Parmesan, if using.

3 Season with salt and pepper and add a squeeze of lemon juice to bring out the flavour. Use immediately, or keep up to two weeks in the fridge.

basic tomato sauce

1 tablespoon olive oil

1 onion, peeled and chopped

2 garlic cloves, peeled

2 x 400g or 14oz cans tomatoes in juice

salt and freshly ground pepper

1 Heat the oil in a large saucepan and add the onion. Cover and cook gently for ten minutes, or until the onions are tender but not brown.

2 Add the garlic, stir well and cook for one to two minutes longer. Stir in the tomatoes, together with their juice, being careful to break up the tomatoes with a wooden spoon.

3 Bring to the boil, then let the mixture simmer for ten to fifteen minutes, until the liquid has disappeared and the sauce is thick.

4 Season with salt and pepper.

basic lentil bolognese

125g or 4oz whole green or brown lentils,
   or split orange lentils, or a 400g
   or 14oz can of green lentils

1 onion, peeled and chopped

2 tablespoons olive oil

2 garlic cloves, peeled and crushed

1 celery stick, chopped

1 carrot, finely diced

2 tomatoes, skinned and chopped

1 teaspoon sun-dried tomato purée

1 tablespoon chopped parsley

salt and freshly ground black pepper

1 If using any dried lentils, put them into a saucepan with 500ml or 18fl oz of water and bring to the boil. Simmer gently until they are tender – forty minutes or so for brown or green lentils, about twenty minutes for the orange ones. Drain the lentils, whether they're the freshly cooked or canned type, reserving the liquid.

2 Fry the onion in the oil for five minutes, then add the garlic, celery and carrot. Cover and leave to cook gently for fifteen minutes until tender, stirring from time to time.

3 Add the lentils, tomatoes, sun-dried tomato purée and enough of the reserved liquid to make a thick, soft consistency. Simmer for about ten minutes, adding more liquid if necessary.

4 Stir in the parsley and season with salt and freshly ground black pepper.

A gourmet who thinks of calories is like a tart who looks at her watch.

James A. Beard

1
creamy pasta

fettuccine with butter & dolcelatte

400g or 14oz fettuccine

salt to taste

55g or 2oz butter

175g or 6oz dolcelatte cheese

freshly ground black pepper

1 Fill a large saucepan with four litres (seven pints) of water and put it on the stove to heat for the pasta.

2 When the water boils, add the pasta along with a teaspoon of salt and give it a quick stir. Briefly put the lid on until it starts to lift, showing that the water has come back to the boil, then let the pasta bubble away, uncovered, for about eight minutes, or until it is tender but still has some bite to it.

3 Just before the pasta is ready, melt the butter in a small saucepan, crumble in the cheese and stir over a gentle heat until it has melted and combined with the butter to make a creamy sauce – do not let it overheat.

4 Drain the pasta by tipping it into a colander placed in the sink, then put it back into the still-warm pan and add the cheese mixture. Grind black pepper over, toss gently and serve on warm plates.

fettuccine with dolcelatte cream sauce & spinach

400g or 14oz fettuccine

salt to taste

1 quantity of cream sauce (page 13)

125g or 4oz dolcelatte, cut into small cubes

125g or 4oz tender spinach leaves,
    finely shredded

freshly ground black pepper

1 tablespoon olive oil, optional

1 Fill a large saucepan with four litres (seven pints) of water and put it on the stove to heat for the pasta.

2 When the water boils, add the pasta along with a teaspoon of salt and give it a quick stir. Briefly put the lid on until it starts to lift, showing that the water has come back to the boil, then let the pasta bubble away, uncovered, for about eight minutes, or until it is tender but still has some bite to it.

3 Heat the cream sauce through gently. Just before the pasta is ready, add the dolcelatte and spinach to the sauce and stir for one to two minutes over the heat. Season with some pepper – it probably will not need any salt because the cheese will have added some.

4 Drain the pasta by tipping it into a colander placed in the sink, then put it back into the still-warm pan. Either add the olive oil to the pasta, serve it on warm plates and spoon the sauce on top; or add the sauce directly to the pasta, toss gently and serve on warm plates.

fettuccine with fresh peas & mint

400g or 14oz fettuccine

salt to taste

450g or 1lb podded tender fresh peas
   or frozen petits pois

1 quantity of cream sauce (page 13)

freshly ground black pepper

1 tablespoon olive oil, optional

2–3 tablespoons chopped fresh mint leaves,
   to serve

1 Fill a large saucepan with four litres (seven pints) of water and put it on the stove to heat for the pasta.

2 When the water boils, add the pasta along with a teaspoon of salt and give it a quick stir. Briefly put the lid on until it starts to lift, showing that the water has come back to the boil, then let the pasta bubble away, uncovered, for about eight minutes, or until it is tender but still has some bite to it.

3 Add the peas to the cream sauce in a pan and cook over a gentle heat to heat through both the peas and the sauce. Check the seasoning, adding a little salt and pepper to taste if it needs it.

4 Drain the pasta by tipping it into a colander placed in the sink, then put it back into the still-warm pan. Either add the olive oil to the pasta, serve it on warm plates and spoon the sauce on top; or add the sauce directly to the pasta, toss gently and serve on warm plates. Scatter the chopped mint on top and serve at once.

fusilli with asparagus & summer herbs

450g or 1lb asparagus, trimmed and cut into
    2.5cm or 1-inch lengths

400g or 14oz fusilli

1 quantity of cream sauce (page 13)

freshly ground black pepper

squeeze of lemon juice, optional

1 tablespoon olive oil

2 tablespoons chopped or torn fresh flat-leaf
    parsley, chervil and chives, to serve

1 Fill a large saucepan with four litres (seven pints) of water and put it on the stove to heat for the pasta.

2 Meanwhile, cook the asparagus in a little boiling water for six to eight minutes, or until tender. Drain the asparagus and keep it warm.

3 When the water in the saucepan boils, add the pasta along with a teaspoon of salt and give it a quick stir. Briefly put the lid on until it starts to lift, showing that the water has come back to the boil, then let the pasta bubble away, uncovered, for about eight minutes, or until it is tender but still has some bite to it.

4 Heat the cream sauce through very gently. Add the asparagus and check the seasoning, adding pepper, a squeeze of lemon juice and salt, if needed.

5 Drain the pasta by tipping it into a colander placed in the sink, then put it back into the still-warm pan. Either add the olive oil to the pasta, serve it on warm plates and spoon the sauce on top; or add the sauce directly to the pasta, toss gently and serve on warm plates. Scatter the herbs on top and serve at once.

pappardelle with porcini mushrooms

400g or 14oz pappardelle

salt to taste

25g or 1oz butter

350g or 12oz fresh porcini mushrooms,
    washed and sliced

1 garlic clove, peeled and crushed

1 quantity of cream sauce (page 13)

squeeze of lemon juice, optional

freshly ground black pepper

1 tablespoon olive oil, optional

sprigs of fresh flat-leaf parsley, to serve

1 Fill a large saucepan with four litres (seven pints) of water and put it on the stove to heat for the pasta.

2 When the water boils, add the pasta, along with a teaspoon of salt, and stir. Cover until the water has come back to the boil, then let the pasta bubble away, uncovered, for about eight minutes, or until tender but still with some bite.

3 Meanwhile, cook the porcini. Melt the butter in a medium saucepan, and add the mushrooms and garlic. Cook for four to five minutes, or until the mushrooms are tender and any remaining liquid has disappeared, stirring from time to time. Keep warm.

4 Heat the cream sauce through gently. Check the seasoning; add a squeeze of lemon juice if needed.

5 Drain the pasta by tipping it into a colander placed in the sink, then put it back into the still-warm pan. Either add the olive oil to the pasta, serve it on warm plates and spoon the sauce on top; or add the sauce directly to the pasta, toss gently and serve on warm plates. Spoon the porcini on top, tear or snip the parsley over, and serve at once.

pasta shells with herbs

400g or 14oz conchiglie

salt to taste

1 quantity of béchamel sauce (page 14)

5–6 tablespoons chopped fresh herbs:
    parsley, chives and chervil, if available

freshly ground black pepper

squeeze of lemon juice, optional

55g or 2oz pine nuts, toasted

1 tablespoon olive oil, optional

sprigs of fresh parsley and flakes of Parmesan
    cheese, to serve

1 Fill a large saucepan with four litres (seven pints) of water and put it on the stove to heat for the pasta.

2 When the water boils, add the pasta along with a teaspoon of salt and give it a quick stir. Briefly put the lid on until it starts to lift, showing that the water has come back to the boil, then let the pasta bubble away, uncovered, for about eight minutes, or until it is tender but still has some bite to it.

3 Meanwhile, heat the béchamel sauce through gently, then stir in the herbs and check the seasoning, adding some grindings of pepper and a squeeze of lemon juice to taste if it needs it.

4 Drain the pasta by tipping it into a colander placed in the sink, then put it back into the still-warm pan. Add the pine nuts to the pan. Either add the olive oil to the pasta, serve it on warm plates and spoon the sauce on top; or add the sauce directly to the pasta, toss gently and serve on warm plates. Decorate with sprigs of parsley and scatter the flakes of Parmesan over the top.

penne with chilli-cream sauce

400g or 14oz penne

salt to taste

1 dried red chilli, crumbled

 tablespoon sun-dried tomato purée

1 quantity of cream sauce (page 13)

freshly ground black pepper

1 tablespoon olive oil, optional

fresh basil leaves, to serve

1 Fill a large saucepan with four litres (seven pints) of water and put it on the stove to heat for the pasta.

2 When the water boils, add the pasta along with a teaspoon of salt and give it a quick stir. Briefly put the lid on until it starts to lift, showing that the water has come back to the boil, then let the pasta bubble away, uncovered, for about eight minutes, or until it is tender but still has some bite to it.

3 Stir the chilli and sun-dried tomato purée into the cream sauce in a pan and heat through gently. Check the seasoning, adding salt and pepper to taste if it needs it.

4 Drain the pasta by tipping it into a colander placed in the sink, then put it back into the still-warm pan. Either add the olive oil to the pasta, serve it on warm plates and spoon the sauce on top; or add the sauce directly to the pasta, toss gently and serve on warm plates. Tear the basil leaves over the top and serve at once.

penne rigate salad with celery, apple & toasted pine nuts

55g or 2oz raisins

400g or 14oz penne rigate

salt to taste

2 sweet apples, diced or sliced, sprinkled with
  lemon juice to preserve the colour

1 tablespoon lemon juice

3 tablespoons mayonnaise

3 tablespoons plain yogurt

freshly ground black pepper

1 celery heart, trimmed and sliced

4 spring onions, trimmed and chopped

125g or 4oz pine nuts, toasted

1 Fill a large saucepan with four litres (seven pints) of water and put it on the stove to heat for the pasta.

2 Meanwhile, put the raisins into a small bowl, cover with boiling water and leave to plump up.

3 When the water in the saucepan boils, add the pasta, along with a teaspoon of salt, and stir. Cover until the water has come back to the boil, then let the pasta bubble away, uncovered, for about eight minutes, or until it is tender but still has some bite to it.

4 Drain the pasta by tipping it into a colander placed in the sink, then put it back into the still-warm pan. Add the mayonnaise, yogurt and some salt and pepper to taste and stir gently until all the pasta is well-coated.

5 Drain the raisins and add to the mixture, along with the apples with their lemon juice, the celery and the spring onions. Check the seasoning, then serve immediately, or cover and leave until the salad cools to room temperature. Either way, scatter with the toasted pine nuts just before serving.

spinach tagliatelle with three cheeses

400g or 14oz spinach tagliatelle (tagliatelle verde)

salt to taste

2 x 125g or 4oz firm goats cheese log,
  each sliced into 4 rounds

1 quantity béchamel sauce (page 14)

55g or 2oz freshly grated Parmesan cheese

freshly ground black pepper

1 tablespoon olive oil

125g or 4oz blue cheese, crumbled

sprigs of flat-leaf parsley, to serve

1 Fill a large saucepan with four litres (seven pints) of water and put it on the stove to heat for the pasta.

2 When the water boils, add the pasta along with a teaspoon of salt and give it a quick stir. Briefly put the lid on until it starts to lift, showing that the water has come back to the boil, then let the pasta bubble away, uncovered, for about eight minutes, or until it is tender but still has some bite to it.

3 Just before the pasta is done, set the grill to high. Line the grill pan with foil and place the rounds of goats cheese on it; grill for three to four minutes until they are golden brown and beginning to melt.

4 Heat the béchamel sauce through gently. Stir in half the Parmesan and check the seasoning, adding salt and pepper as necessary.

5 Drain the pasta by tipping it into a colander placed in the sink, then put it back into the still-warm pan. Add the olive oil and toss gently. Serve the pasta on warmed plates, spoon the sauce on top, then scatter with the blue cheese and remaining Parmesan and place two circles of goats cheese on each serving. Garnish with a few sprigs of flat-leaf parsley.

tagliatelle with gruyère, parmesan & parsley

400g or 14oz tagliatelle

salt to taste

1 quantity of cream sauce (page 13)

100g or 3½oz Gruyère, grated

55g or 2oz freshly grated Parmesan cheese

1 tablespoon olive oil, optional

freshly ground black pepper

sprigs of fresh parsley, preferably flat-leaf, to serve

1 Fill a large saucepan with four litres (seven pints) of water and put it on the stove to heat for the pasta.

2 When the water boils, add the pasta along with a teaspoon of salt and give it a quick stir. Briefly put the lid on until it starts to lift, showing that the water has come back to the boil, then let the pasta bubble away, uncovered, for about eight minutes, or until it is tender but still has some bite to it.

3 Heat the cream sauce through gently. Just before the pasta is done, add all the Gruyère and half of the Parmesan to the sauce.

4 Drain the pasta by tipping it into a colander placed in the sink, then put it back into the still-warm pan. Either add the olive oil to the pasta, serve it on warm plates and spoon the sauce on top; or add the sauce directly to the pasta, toss gently and serve on warm plates. Coarsely grind some black pepper to taste over the pasta, scatter with the remaining Parmesan and tear the sprigs of parsley over the top. Serve at once.

tagliatelle with stilton & pecans

400g or 14oz tagliatelle, plain or verde

salt to taste

8 tablespoons single cream or pasta
cooking water

1 garlic clove, peeled and crushed

175g or 6oz Stilton cheese

freshly ground black pepper

55g or 2oz pecans, roughly chopped, toasted

1 Fill a large saucepan with four litres (seven pints) of water and put it on the stove to heat for the pasta.

2 When the water boils, add the pasta along with a teaspoon of salt and give it a quick stir. Briefly put the lid on until it starts to lift, showing that the water has come back to the boil, then let the pasta bubble away, uncovered, for about eight minutes, or until it is tender but still has some bite to it.

3 Just before the pasta is ready, heat the cream (or the same quantity of water, scooped from the pasta pan) in a small saucepan, add the garlic and crumble in the Stilton. Stir over a gentle heat until the cheese has melted and combined with the liquid to make a creamy sauce – do not let it overheat.

4 Drain the pasta by tipping it into a colander placed in the sink, then put it back into the still-warm pan and add the cheese mixture. Grind black pepper over, toss gently and serve on warm plates, scattered with the toasted pecans.

There are five elements:
earth, air, fire, water – and garlic.

Louis Diat

2

garlicky pasta

buttery spaghetti
with lemon & parmesan

500g or 1lb 2oz spaghetti

55g or 2oz soft (but not melted) butter

100g or 3½oz Parmesan cheese, finely grated

grated rind and juice of 1 unwaxed lemon

2 garlic cloves, crushed

salt and freshly ground black pepper

1 Fill a large saucepan with four litres (seven pints) of water and put it on the stove to heat for the pasta.

2 When the water boils, add the spaghetti, holding it straight up like a bunch of flowers and gently pushing it into the water as it softens. Add teaspoon of salt and give it a quick stir. Briefly put the lid on until it starts to lift, showing that the water has come back to the boil, then let the pasta bubble away, uncovered, for about eight minutes, or until it is tender but still has some bite to it.

2 While the spaghetti is cooking, put the butter into a small bowl and mix in the grated cheese, lemon rind and juice. Set aside.

3 When the spaghetti is done to your liking, drain it and put back into the pan. Add the lemony mixture along with some salt and pepper and swirl around so that all the spaghetti is coated, then serve immediately.

fettuccine with lemon

400g or 14oz fettuccine

salt to taste

1 fat, juicy garlic clove, peeled and crushed

2–4 tablespoons olive oil

finely grated or thinly pared rind of 1 lemon

juice of 1 lemon

freshly ground black pepper

freshly torn flat-leaf parsley, to serve, optional

freshly grated Parmesan cheese, to serve, optional

1 Fill a large saucepan with four litres (seven pints) of water and put it on the stove to heat for the pasta.

2 When the water boils, add the pasta along with a teaspoon of salt and give it a quick stir. Briefly put the lid on until it starts to lift, showing that the water has come back to the boil, then let the pasta bubble away, uncovered, for about eight minutes, or until it is tender but still has some bite to it.

3 Meanwhile, cook the garlic in the olive oil over a gentle heat for two to three minutes, without letting it brown. Keep on one side.

4 Drain the pasta by tipping it into a colander placed in the sink, then put it back into the still-warm pan. Add the garlic and its oil, the lemon rind and juice, and plenty of black pepper. Toss gently, then serve on warm plates with parsley and Parmesan on top, if using.

fettuccine with mint pesto & sugar-snap peas

500g or 1lb 2oz fettucine

250g or 9oz sugar-snap peas

1 tablespoon roughly chopped mint

salt and freshly ground black pepper

flaked or grated Parmesan to serve, optional

for the mint pesto

handful of mint, stalks removed

2 garlic cloves, crushed

4 tablespoons olive oil

1 Bring a large saucepan of water to the boil, put in the pasta and a teaspoon of salt and boil until it's almost, but not quite, tender. Add the peas and cook for a further two to three minutes, or until the pasta is *al dente* and the peas are tender. Drain and return to the pan.

2 While the pasta is cooking, make the mint pesto by whizzing the mint, garlic and olive oil in a food processor until you have a green purée.

3 Stir the mint pesto into the pasta mixture, along with the roughly chopped mint, and salt and pepper to taste. Toss the mixture gently until it's evenly coated with the mint pesto, then serve immediately, with Parmesan, if desired.

fettuccine with sun-dried tomatoes & basil

400g or 14oz fettuccine

salt to taste

2–4 fat, juicy garlic cloves, peeled and sliced

2–4 tablespoons olive oil or oil from the
    sun-dried tomatoes

12 sun-dried tomatoes, chopped

freshly ground black pepper

fresh basil leaves

flakes of Parmesan cheese, to serve

1 Fill a large saucepan with four litres (seven pints) of water and put it on the stove to heat for the pasta.

2 When the water boils, add the pasta along with a teaspoon of salt and give it a quick stir. Briefly put the lid on until it starts to lift, showing that the water has come back to the boil, then let the pasta bubble away, uncovered, for about eight minutes, or until it is tender but still has some bite to it.

3 Meanwhile, cook the garlic in the olive or sun-dried tomato oil over a gentle heat – it needs just to soften and warm through without going brown. Just before the pasta is done, add the sun-dried tomatoes to the garlic mixture and warm them through.

4 Drain the pasta by tipping it into a colander placed in the sink, then put it back into the still-warm pan. Add the garlic mixture and salt and pepper to taste, toss gently and serve on warm plates. Tear the basil over and scatter the Parmesan on top.

fusilli with garlic & herb cream cheese

400g or 14oz fusilli

salt to taste

225g or 8oz podded fresh young peas or
frozen petits pois

150g or 5½oz garlic and herb cream cheese,
full-fat or reduced fat

1 Fill a large saucepan with four litres (seven pints) of water and put it on the stove to heat for the pasta.

2 When the water in the saucepan boils, add the pasta along with a teaspoon of salt and give it a quick stir. Briefly put the lid on until it starts to lift, showing that the water has come back to the boil, then let the pasta bubble away, uncovered, for about eight minutes, or until it is tender but still has some bite to it.

3 Just before the pasta is done, add the peas to it and cook briefly, just enough to heat the peas through.

4 Drain the pasta and peas by tipping them into a colander placed in the sink, then put them back into the still-warm pan with the cream cheese. Toss gently and serve on warm plates.

fusilli lunghi with nut pesto

400g or 14oz fusilli lunghi

salt to taste

fresh parsley, preferably flat-leaf, to serve

for the pesto
55g or 2oz walnuts, pecans or cashews, toasted

2 tablespoons pine nuts, toasted

2 garlic cloves, peeled

1 tablespoon soy sauce

4 tablespoons olive oil

salt and freshly ground black pepper

squeeze of lemon juice, optional

1 Fill a large saucepan with four litres (seven pints) of water and put it on the stove to heat for the pasta.

2 Meanwhile, make the pesto; this can be done in advance if you prefer. Follow the recipe on page 16, leaving out the Parmesan and using the nuts instead of the basil, only four tablespoons of oil, a tablespoon of soy sauce and three tablespoons of water.

3 When the water in the saucepan boils, add the pasta, along with a teaspoon of salt, and stir. Cover until the water has come back to the boil, then let the pasta bubble away, uncovered, for about eight minutes, or until *al dente*.

4 Scoop up about half a mugful of water from the pasta and set aside. Drain the pasta by tipping it into a colander placed in the sink, then put it back into the still-warm pan. Give the pesto a stir and loosen it a bit, if it needs it, by mixing in a couple of tablespoons of the hot pasta water, then add it to the pasta. Toss the pasta gently until it is all coated with the pesto, check the seasoning, then serve at once on warm plates. Tear or snip the parsley over the top.

middle-eastern spiced lentil & pasta soup

3 tablespoons olive oil

2 onions, peeled and chopped

2 garlic cloves, peeled and crushed

125g or 4oz split red lentils

1.2 litres or 40fl oz vegetable stock

55g or 2oz small pasta shapes

1 tablespoon ground coriander

1 tablespoon ground cumin

squeeze of lemon juice

salt and freshly ground black pepper

4 tablespoons roughly chopped fresh
coriander, to serve

1 Heat the oil in a large saucepan, put in the onion and garlic, stir briefly, then cover and leave to cook gently for ten minutes, or until the onion is becoming soft. Transfer about a third of the mixture to a smaller saucepan and leave on one side.

2 Add the lentils and the stock to the onions in the large saucepan. Bring to the boil, then lower the heat and leave to simmer for thirty minutes. Add the pasta and cook for a further eight minutes.

3 In the meantime, reheat the onion and garlic in the smaller saucepan, then stir in the coriander and cumin. Cook for one minute, stirring constantly, then remove from the heat and add to the soup, along with a squeeze of lemon juice and salt and pepper to taste.

4 Serve the soup in warm bowls and top each with a good spoonful of chopped fresh coriander.

penne with chilli pesto

400g or 14oz penne

salt to taste

for the pesto
55g or 2oz fresh basil leaves

2 garlic cloves, peeled

2 tablespoons pine nuts, toasted

1–2 fresh green chillies, deseeded

8 tablespoons olive oil

salt and freshly ground black pepper

squeeze of lemon juice, optional

1 Fill a large saucepan with four litres (seven pints) of water and put it on the stove to heat for the pasta.

2 Meanwhile, make the pesto, or this can be done well in advance if you prefer. Follow the recipe on page 16, pulverizing the chillies along with the basil and the other ingredients and leaving out the Parmesan cheese.

3 When the water in the saucepan boils, add the pasta along with a teaspoon of salt and give it a quick stir. Briefly put the lid on until it starts to lift, showing that the water has come back to the boil, then let the pasta bubble away, uncovered, for about eight minutes, or until it is tender but still has some bite to it.

4 Scoop up half a mugful of water from the pasta and set aside. Drain the pasta into a colander placed in the sink, then put it back into the still-warm pan. Loosen the pesto, if it needs it, by mixing in a couple of tablespoons of the hot pasta water, then add it to the pasta. Toss the pasta gently until well-coated with the pesto, check the seasoning, then serve at once on warm plates.

pennoni with broccoli, mascarpone, garlic & fresh basil

400g or 14oz pennoni

salt to taste

450g or 1lb prepared broccoli,
cut into 1cm or ½-inch pieces

1 garlic clove, peeled and crushed

1 tablespoon olive oil

125g or 4oz mascarpone cheese

freshly ground black pepper

fresh basil leaves, to serve

1 Fill a large saucepan with four litres (seven pints) of water and put it on the stove to heat for the pasta.

2 When the water boils, add the pasta along with a teaspoon of salt and give it a quick stir. Briefly put the lid on until it starts to lift, showing that the water has come back to the boil, then let the pasta bubble away, uncovered, for about eight minutes, or until it is tender but still has some bite to it.

3 Meanwhile, cook the broccoli in a little boiling water for three to four minutes, or until just tender, then drain and keep warm.

4 Cook the garlic in the olive oil over a gentle heat for two to three minutes, without letting it brown. Keep to one side.

5 Drain the pasta by tipping it into a colander placed in the sink, then put it back into the still-warm pan with the garlic, along with its oil, stirring gently so that the oil coats the pasta. Add the mascarpone and broccoli, check the seasoning and serve on warm plates. Tear the basil over the top.

pipe rigate with red peppers & garlic

4 red peppers, quartered

400g or 14oz pipe rigate

salt to taste

2 fat, juicy garlic cloves, peeled and thinly sliced

2 tablespoons olive oil

freshly ground black pepper

fresh basil leaves, to serve

1 Fill a large saucepan with four litres (seven pints) of water and put it on the stove to heat for the pasta.

2 Next, prepare the peppers by placing them skin-side up on a grill pan. Put under a high heat for ten to fifteen minutes, or until the skin has blistered and blackened in places. Cover with a plate and leave until cool enough to handle, then remove the skin, stem and seeds. Cut the flesh into strips.

3 When the water in the saucepan boils, add the pasta along with a teaspoon of salt and stir. Briefly put the lid on until it starts to lift, showing that the water has come back to the boil, then let the pasta bubble away, uncovered, for about eight minutes, or until it is tender but still has some bite.

4 Meanwhile, cook the garlic in the olive oil over a gentle heat for two to three minutes, without letting it brown. Keep on one side.

5 Drain the pasta by tipping it into a colander placed in the sink, then put it back into the still-warm pan. Add the olive oil and garlic, along with the pepper strips, and toss gently. Add salt and pepper to taste and serve on warm plates. Tear the basil over the top.

spaghetti with garlic & olive oil

400g or 14oz spaghetti

salt to taste

2–4 fat, juicy garlic cloves, peeled and sliced,
chopped or crushed

2–4 tablespoons olive oil

freshly ground black pepper

freshly grated Parmesan cheese, to serve, optional

1 Fill a large saucepan with four litres (seven pints) of water and put it on the stove to heat for the pasta.

2 When the water boils, add the spaghetti, holding it straight up like a bunch of flowers and gently pushing it into the water as it softens. Add a teaspoon of salt and give it a quick stir. Briefly put the lid on until it starts to lift, showing that the water has come back to the boil, then let the pasta bubble away, uncovered, for about eight minutes, or until it is tender but still has some bite to it.

3 Meanwhile, cook the garlic in the olive oil over a gentle heat; it needs just to soften and warm through without going brown.

4 Drain the pasta by tipping it into a colander placed in the sink, then put it back into the still-warm pan. Add the garlic and its oil, along with a good grinding of salt and pepper as needed, toss gently and serve on warm plates. Hand round the Parmesan, if desired.

spaghetti with garlic, olive oil & chilli

400g or 14oz spaghetti

4 tablespoons olive oil

3 fat garlic cloves, chopped

½–1 teaspoon red chilli flakes

salt and freshly ground black pepper

freshly grated Parmesan or pecorino cheese,
  to serve, optional

1 Fill a large saucepan with four litres (seven pints) of water and put it on the stove to heat for the pasta.

2 When the water boils, add the spaghetti, holding it straight up like a bunch of flowers and gently pushing it into the water as it softens. Add a teaspoon of salt and give it a quick stir. Briefly put the lid on until it starts to lift, showing that the water has come back to the boil, then let the pasta bubble away, uncovered, for about eight minutes, or until it is tender but still has some bite to it.

2 While it's cooking, heat the oil, put in the garlic and cook gently for about two minutes – don't let it brown at all. Set aside.

3 When the spaghetti is done to your liking, drain it and put back into the pan. Quickly reheat the garlic and oil mixture, then tip it into the spaghetti, along with a sprinkling of red chilli flakes and some salt and pepper. Toss gently.

4 Serve at once, with Parmesan or pecorino if desired.

spaghetti with homemade pesto

400g or 14oz spaghetti

salt and freshly ground black pepper

flaked or grated Parmesan to serve, optional

for the pesto
55g or 2oz fresh basil

25g or 1oz pine nuts

55g or 2oz finely grated Parmesan or
    pecorino cheese

2 garlic cloves, crushed

4 tablespoons olive oil

1 Fill a large saucepan with four litres (seven pints) of water and put it on the stove to heat for the pasta.

2 When the water boils, add the spaghetti, holding it straight up like a bunch of flowers and then gently pushing it into the water as it softens. Add a teaspoon of salt and give it a quick stir. Briefly put the lid on until it starts to lift, showing that the water has come back to boiling point, then let the pasta bubble away, uncovered, for about eight minutes, or until it is tender but still has some bite to it. Save a few tablespoons of the water in case you want to thin the pesto.

2 While the spaghetti is cooking, make the pesto: put all the ingredients into a blender or food processor and whizz until you have a glossy green purée. If it's a bit thick, thin it with a tablespoonful or two of the hot pasta water.

3 Stir the pesto into the pasta mixture, along with salt and pepper to taste. Toss gently until the spaghetti is coated with the pesto. Serve immediately, with Parmesan if desired.

spaghetti with olive oil & red chilli flakes

400g or 14oz spaghetti

salt to taste

2 garlic cloves, peeled and finely chopped

2–4 tablespoons olive oil

1–2 dried red chillies, crumbled

freshly ground black pepper

fresh Parmesan, flaked or grated,
    to serve, optional

torn or chopped fresh flat-leaf parsley,
    to serve, optional

1 Fill a large saucepan with four litres (seven pints) of water and put it on the stove to heat for the pasta.

2 When the water in the saucepan boils, add the spaghetti, holding it straight up like a bunch of flowers and gently pushing it into the water as it softens. Add a teaspoon of salt and give it a quick stir. Briefly put the lid on until it starts to lift, showing that the water has come back to the boil, then let the pasta bubble away, uncovered, for about eight minutes, or until it is tender but still has some bite.

3 Just before the pasta is done, cook the garlic in the olive oil over a gentle heat for two to three minutes without letting it brown. Then add the chilli (stand back, as the oil released by chilli on contact with heat can make you cough) and stir-fry for a few seconds. Leave to one side until the spaghetti is done.

4 Drain the pasta by tipping it into a colander placed in the sink, then put it back into the still-warm pan. Quickly reheat the garlic mixture, then pour it onto the pasta. Stir gently, season with salt and pepper, then serve it on warm plates and top with some Parmesan and/or parsley.

spaghetti with red-pepper pesto & black olives

400g or 14oz spaghetti

handful of Kalamata black olives

salt and freshly ground black pepper

freshly grated Parmesan or pecorino, to serve

for the pesto
1 large red pepper, halved and deseeded

2 garlic cloves, crushed

pinch red chilli flakes (or to taste)

4 tablespoons olive oil

salt and freshly ground black pepper

1 Fill a large saucepan with four litres (seven pints) of water and put it on the stove to heat for the pasta.

2 When the water boils, add the spaghetti, holding it straight up like a bunch of flowers and gently pushing it into the water as it softens. Add a teaspoon of salt and give it a quick stir. Cover until the water has come back to the boil, then let the pasta bubble away, uncovered, for about eight minutes, or until it is tender but still has some bite to it. Drain and return to the pan.

3 Meanwhile, place the pepper halves cut-side down on a grill pan and leave under a high grill for about ten minutes, or until tender and blackened in places. Remove from the heat, strip off any very blackened bits of skin.

4 Whizz the red pepper in a food processor or blender with the crushed garlic, chilli flakes, olive oil and some salt and pepper.

5 Add the pesto and the olives to the drained spaghetti in the pan and swirl them around, adding salt and pepper to taste, then serve on warmed plates. Offer Parmesan or pecorino separately.

tagliatelle with green peppercorns

400g or 14oz tagliatelle

salt to taste

2–4 tablespoons olive oil

1 tablespoon green peppercorns

freshly ground black pepper

freshly chopped parsley or chervil, to serve

freshly grated Parmesan or pecorino cheese,
    to serve

1 Fill a large saucepan with four litres (seven pints) of water and put it on the stove to heat for the pasta.

2 When the water boils, add the pasta along with a teaspoon of salt and give it a quick stir. Briefly put the lid on until it starts to lift, showing that the water has come back to the boil, then let the pasta bubble away, uncovered, for about eight minutes, or until it is tender but still has some bite to it.

3 Drain the pasta by tipping it into a colander placed in the sink, then put it back into the still-warm pan, add the olive oil, green peppercorns and salt and black pepper to taste, toss gently and serve on warm plates, with the herbs and cheese scattered over the top.

tagliatelle with lentil & wine sauce

400g or 14oz tagliatelle

salt to taste

1 glass of red wine

1 quantity of lentil bolognese sauce (page 18)

freshly ground black pepper

1 tablespoon olive oil, optional

fresh basil leaves, to serve

flakes of Parmesan cheese, to serve

1 Fill a large saucepan with four litres (seven pints) of water and put it on the stove to heat for the pasta.

2 When the water boils, add the pasta along with a teaspoon of salt and give it a quick stir. Briefly put the lid on until it starts to lift, showing that the water has come back to the boil, then let the pasta bubble away, uncovered, for about eight minutes, or until it is tender but still has some bite to it.

3 Meanwhile, add the wine to the bolognese sauce in a pan, bring to the boil, then let simmer gently. Check the seasoning, adding salt and pepper to taste, if needed.

4 Drain the pasta by tipping it into a colander placed in the sink, then put it back into the still-warm pan. Either add the olive oil to the pasta, serve it on warm plates and spoon the sauce on top; or add the sauce directly to the pasta, toss gently and serve on warm plates. Tear basil leaves over the top, scatter with flakes of Parmesan and serve at once.

tagliatelle with rocket pesto & pine nuts

400g or 14oz tagliatelle

25g or 1oz pine nuts, toasted

salt and freshly ground black pepper

flaked pecorino, to serve

for the rocket pesto
55g or 2oz rocket

25g or 1oz pine nuts, raw or toasted

55g or 2oz finely grated Parmesan or
    pecorino cheese

2 garlic cloves, crushed

4 tablespoons olive oil

1 Fill a large saucepan with four litres (seven pints) of water and put it on the stove to heat for the pasta.

2 When the water boils, add the pasta along with a teaspoon of salt and give it a quick stir. Briefly put the lid on until it starts to lift, showing that the water has come back to the boil, then let the pasta bubble away, uncovered, for about eight minutes, or until it is tender but still has some bite to it.

3 While the tagliatelle is cooking, make the pesto: put all the ingredients into a blender or food processor and whizz until you have a glossy green purée – pesto. If it's a bit thick, thin it with a tablespoonful or two of the hot pasta water.

4 Drain the pasta and return it to the pan. Stir the pesto into the pasta mixture, along with the toasted pine nuts, salt and pepper to taste. Toss gently until the tagliatelle is coated with the pesto and serve immediately, scattered with flakes of cheese.

tagliatelle with walnuts & walnut oil

400g or 14oz tagliatelle

salt to taste

1 garlic clove, peeled and crushed

1 tablespoon olive oil

2 tablespoons walnut oil

125–175g or 4–6oz shelled walnuts
(preferably freshly cracked), roughly chopped

freshly ground black pepper

freshly chopped parsley, to serve, optional

fresh Parmesan cheese, cut in flakes or grated,
to serve optional

1 Fill a large saucepan with four litres (seven pints) of water and put it on the stove to heat for the pasta.

2 When the water boils, add the pasta along with a teaspoon of salt and give it a quick stir. Briefly put the lid on until it starts to lift, showing that the water has come back to the boil, then let the pasta bubble away, uncovered, for about eight minutes, or until it is tender but still has some bite to it.

3 Meanwhile, cook the garlic in the olive oil over a gentle heat for two to three minutes, without letting it brown. Keep to one side.

4 Drain the pasta by tipping it into a colander placed in the sink, then put it back into the still-warm pan. Add the olive oil and garlic mixture, the walnut oil and walnuts, and grind over black pepper to taste. Toss gently, then serve on warm plates, with parsley and Parmesan on top, if using.

tuscan white bean & pasta soup

olive oil

1 onion, peeled and chopped

2 garlic cloves, peeled and crushed

2 x 400g or 14oz cans cannellini beans

1.2 litres or 40fl oz vegetable stock

4 thick slices of bread, crusts removed

55g or 2oz small pasta shapes

salt and freshly ground black pepper

croûtons, optional

1 Heat two tablespoons of olive oil in a large saucepan, put in the onion and half the garlic, stir briefly, then cover and leave to cook gently for ten minutes, until the onion is becoming soft.

2 Add the beans, together with their liquid, and the stock. Bring to the boil, then lower the heat and leave to simmer for twenty minutes.

3 Meanwhile, make the croûtons. Rub the surface of the bread with the remaining garlic, then fry the bread on both sides in a little hot olive oil, until crisp and golden. Cut into small squares and keep to one side.

4 Add the pasta shapes to the soup, bring back to the boil and simmer for six to eight minutes, or until the pasta is cooked. Season with salt and pepper, then serve into warmed bowls and top each with some croûtons.

Nature alone is antique and the oldest art a mushroom.

Thomas Carlyle

3
mushroomy pasta

farfalle with mushrooms, peas & parsley

400g or 14oz farfalle

salt to taste

350g or 12oz mushrooms, washed and sliced

25g or 1oz butter

1 tablespoon olive oil

1 garlic clove, peeled and crushed

225g or 8oz podded fresh peas, frozen petits pois
or trimmed mange-tout

2 tablespoons chopped fresh parsley, flat-leaf if
available, to serve

1 Fill a large saucepan with four litres (seven pints) of water and put it on the stove to heat for the pasta.

2 When the water boils, add the pasta along with a teaspoon of salt and give it a quick stir. Briefly put the lid on until it starts to lift, showing that the water has come back to the boil, then let the pasta bubble away, uncovered, for about eight minutes, or until it is tender but still has some bite to it.

3 Fry the mushrooms and garlic in the butter and olive oil for four to five minutes, until tender and any liquid has boiled away.

4 Just before the pasta is thoroughly cooked, add the peas (or mange-tout) to it and cook briefly, just to heat them through.

5 Drain the pasta and peas by tipping them into a colander placed in the sink, then put them back into the still-warm pan, add the mushrooms, toss gently and serve on warm plates with the parsley on top.

farfalle with shiitake mushrooms, parmesan & sage

400g or 14oz farfalle

salt to taste

450g or 1lb fresh shiitake mushrooms, washed and sliced

2 tablespoons olive oil

1 garlic clove, peeled and crushed

6 fresh sage leaves, chopped

freshly ground black pepper

55g or 2oz freshly flaked Parmesan cheese

1 Fill a large saucepan with four litres (seven pints) of water and put it on the stove to heat for the pasta.

2 When the water boils, add the pasta along with a teaspoon of salt and give it a quick stir. Briefly put the lid on until it starts to lift, showing that the water has come back to the boil, then let the pasta bubble away, uncovered, for about eight minutes, or until it is tender but still has some bite to it.

3 Meanwhile, fry the mushrooms and garlic in the olive oil for four to five minutes, or until tender and any liquid has boiled away. Stir in the sage and season with salt and pepper.

4 Drain the pasta by tipping it into a colander placed in the sink, then put it back into the still-warm pan. Add the mushroom and sage mixture and Parmesan, toss gently and serve on warm plates.

fusilli lunghi with mushrooms in lentil bolognese sauce

400g or 14oz fusilli lunghi

salt to taste

225g or 8oz mushrooms, washed and sliced

olive oil

2 garlic cloves, peeled and crushed

1 quantity of lentil bolognese sauce (page 18)

freshly ground black pepper

fresh Parmesan cheese, flaked or grated, to serve

1 Fill a large saucepan with four litres (seven pints) of water and put it on the stove to heat for the pasta.

2 When the water boils, add the pasta along with a teaspoon of salt and give it a quick stir. Briefly put the lid on until it starts to lift, showing that the water has come back to the boil, then let the pasta bubble away, uncovered, for about eight minutes, or until it is tender but still has some bite to it.

3 Fry the mushrooms with the garlic in one tablespoon of olive oil for four to five minutes until tender and any liquid has boiled away.

4 Add the mushrooms to the bolognese sauce in a pan and heat through gently. Check the seasoning, adding salt and pepper to taste, if needed.

5 Drain the pasta by tipping it into a colander placed in the sink, then put it back into the still-warm pan. Either add one tablespoon of olive oil to the pasta, serve it on warm plates and spoon the sauce on top; or add the sauce directly to the pasta, toss gently and serve on warm plates. Serve at once and hand around the Parmesan.

gnocchi with mushrooms, artichokes, mascarpone & fresh basil

400g or 14oz gnocchi

salt to taste

350g or 12oz mushrooms, washed and sliced

1 tablespoon olive oil

1 garlic clove, peeled and crushed

400g or 14oz can artichoke hearts, drained
  and sliced

125g or 4oz mascarpone cheese, or reduced-fat
  cream cheese

freshly ground black pepper

fresh basil leaves, to serve

1 Fill a large saucepan with four litres (seven pints) of water and put it on the stove to heat for the pasta.

2 When the water boils, add the pasta along with a teaspoon of salt and give it a quick stir. Briefly put the lid on until it starts to lift, showing that the water has come back to the boil, then let the pasta bubble away, uncovered, for about eight minutes, or until it is tender but still has some bite to it.

3 Fry the mushrooms and garlic in the olive oil for four to five minutes until tender and any liquid has boiled away. Add the artichoke hearts and continue to cook gently until they are heated through.

4 Drain the pasta by tipping it into a colander placed in the sink, then put it back into the still-warm pan with the mascarpone and stir gently until the cheese has heated through but not boiled. Add the mushroom and artichoke mixture, mix gently and season with salt and pepper. Serve immediately on warm plates with a generous amount of fresh basil torn or snipped over the top.

lasagnette with mascarpone & mushrooms

400g or 14oz lasagnette

salt to taste

25g or 1oz butter

450g or 1lb mushrooms, washed and sliced

2 garlic cloves, peeled and crushed

125g or 4oz mascarpone cheese
   (or low-fat cream cheese)

1 quantity of tomato sauce (page 17)

freshly ground black pepper

1 tablespoon olive oil, optional

fresh basil leaves, to serve

flakes of Parmesan cheese, to serve

1 Fill a large saucepan with four litres (seven pints) of water and put it on the stove to heat for the pasta.

2 When the water boils, add the pasta, along with a teaspoon of salt, and stir. Cover until the water has come back to the boil, then let the pasta bubble away, uncovered, for about eight minutes, or until it is tender but still has some bite to it.

3 Meanwhile, cook the mushrooms. Melt the butter in a medium saucepan, add the mushrooms and garlic and cook for four to five minutes, or until tender and any liquid has disappeared, stirring occasionally.

4 Add the mascarpone to the tomato sauce in a pan and heat through gently, stirring until the cheese has melted. Add the mushrooms and check the seasoning, adjusting if necessary.

5 Drain the pasta, then put it back into the still-warm pan. Either add the olive oil to the pasta, serve it on warm plates and spoon the sauce on top; or add the sauce directly to the pasta, toss gently and serve on warm plates. Tear some basil leaves over, scatter with Parmesan and serve immediately.

lumache with wild mushrooms

400g or 14oz lumache

salt to taste

450–675g or 1–1½lb wild mushrooms,
    washed and sliced

2 tablespoons olive oil

2 garlic cloves, peeled and crushed

squeeze of lemon juice

freshly ground black pepper

roughly chopped fresh parsley, preferably flat-leaf,
    to serve, optional

fresh Parmesan cheese, flaked or grated, to serve

1 Fill a large saucepan with four litres (seven pints) of water and put it on the stove to heat for the pasta.

2 When the water boils, add the pasta along with a teaspoon of salt and give it a quick stir. Briefly put the lid on until it starts to lift, showing that the water has come back to the boil, then let the pasta bubble away, uncovered, for about eight minutes, or until it is tender but still has some bite to it.

3 Meanwhile, fry the mushrooms and garlic in the olive oil for four to five minutes until tender and any liquid has boiled away. Add a squeeze of lemon juice to bring out the flavour, then season with salt and pepper.

4 Drain the pasta by tipping it into a colander placed in the sink, then put it back into the still-warm pan, add the mushrooms, toss gently and check the seasoning, adding more salt and pepper if necessary. Serve on warm plates, and scatter the parsley and Parmesan, if using, over the top.

mushroom & garlic cream cheese lasagne

2 tablespoons olive oil

1 onion, peeled and finely chopped

675g or 1½lb mushrooms, washed and sliced

1 large garlic clove, peeled and crushed

225g or 8oz full-fat or reduced-fat garlic
cream cheese

salt and freshly ground black pepper

150–175g or 5½–6oz oven-ready lasagne verde

2 quantities of tomato sauce (page 17)

55g or 2oz freshly grated Parmesan cheese

1 Preheat the oven to 200°C (400°F or gas mark 6). Grease a casserole dish or roasting tin measuring about 20cm x 30cm (8 x 12 inches) and at least 6cm (2½ inches) deep.

2 Heat the oil in a medium-sized saucepan and fry the onion, covered, for five minutes. Add the sliced mushrooms to the onion, along with the garlic, and fry for a further five to ten minutes, or until the mushrooms are tender and any liquid they have produced has boiled away. Remove the pan from the heat, stir in the cream cheese and season with salt and pepper.

3 Rinse the ready-to-use lasagne sheets under the cold tap, then arrange sheets of lasagne in the base of the dish, to cover it. On top of this, put first a layer of tomato sauce, then half the mushroom sauce, followed by a layer of lasagne and another of tomato sauce. Top this with the remaining mushroom mixture, the rest of the lasagne and a final layer of tomato sauce. Scatter the Parmesan on top.

4 Bake the lasagne for thirty-five to forty minutes, or until the pasta is tender and the top golden brown.

orecchiette with oyster mushrooms

225g or 8oz leeks, trimmed and cut into 5mm
or ¼-inch slices

2 tablespoons olive oil, or oil from the
sun-dried tomatoes

400g or 14oz orecchiette

salt to taste

225g or 8oz oyster mushrooms, washed and sliced

8 sun-dried tomatoes, chopped

freshly ground black pepper

fresh basil leaves

flakes of Parmesan cheese, to serve

1 Fill a large saucepan with four litres (seven pints) of water and put it on the stove to heat for the pasta.

2 Meanwhile, cook the leeks – either sauté in one tablespoon of oil or, for a less rich result, in a little boiling water. Either way, they will take about six minutes. Drain the leeks, if necessary, and keep them warm.

3 When the water in the saucepan boils, add the pasta along with a teaspoon of salt and give it a quick stir. Cover until the water has come back to the boil, then let the pasta bubble away, uncovered, for about eight minutes, or until *al dente*.

4 Meanwhile, heat the remaining oil in a saucepan and fry the mushrooms for four to five minutes until tender.

5 Drain the pasta by tipping it into a colander placed in the sink, then put it back into the still-warm pan. Add the leeks, the mushrooms with their oil, sun-dried tomatoes and a seasoning of salt and pepper to taste. Serve the pasta on warm plates, tear the basil over and scatter the Parmesan on top.

tagliatelle with creamy mushroom sauce

400g or 14oz tagliatelle

500g or 1lb 2oz closed-cap white mushrooms

2 tablespoons olive oil

15g or ½oz butter

4 fat garlic cloves, sliced

2 teaspoons cornflour

150ml or 5fl oz double cream

salt and freshly ground black pepper

freshly grated nutmeg

1 Fill a large saucepan with four litres (seven pints) of water and put it on the stove to heat for the pasta.

2 Wash the mushrooms, pat dry on kitchen paper, then quarter them. Heat one tablespoonful of the oil and the butter in a saucepan, put in the mushrooms and garlic and cook gently for about five minutes, or until the mushrooms are tender. There may be some liquid in the pan; that's all right.

3 Sprinkle in the cornflour, mix away any lumps, then pour in the cream, still stirring. Let the mixture come to the boil and thicken a little, then remove from the heat, season with salt, pepper and nutmeg and leave to one side.

4 Put the pasta into the boiling water, along with a teaspoon of salt, and let it come back to the boil, then cook for six to eight minutes, or until *al dente*. Drain, return to the saucepan with the remaining tablespoonful of olive oil and toss gently with some salt to taste.

5 Reheat the mushroom sauce and either pour it into the cooked pasta and mix gently, or serve the pasta on plates and spoon the sauce on top.

tagliatelle in mushroom & garlic sauce

400g or 14oz tagliatelle

salt to taste

25g or 1oz butter

450g or 1lb mushrooms, washed and sliced

2 garlic cloves, peeled and crushed

1 quantity of béchamel sauce (page 14)

freshly ground black pepper

squeeze of lemon juice, optional

1 tablespoon olive oil, optional

bunch of fresh flat-leaf parsley

freshly grated Parmesan cheese, to serve

1 Fill a large saucepan with four litres (seven pints) of water and put it on the stove to heat for the pasta.

2 When the water boils, add the pasta along with a teaspoon of salt and stir. Cover until the water has come back to the boil, then let the pasta bubble away, uncovered, for about eight minutes, or until it is tender but still has some bite to it.

3 Meanwhile, cook the mushrooms. Melt the butter in a medium saucepan, add the mushrooms and garlic and cook for four to five minutes, or until tender and any liquid has disappeared, stirring from time to time.

4 Gently reheat the béchamel, stir in the mushrooms and check the seasoning; adjust, if needed.

5 Drain the tagliatelle by tipping it into a colander placed in the sink, then put it back into the still-warm pan. Either add the olive oil to the pasta, serve it on warm plates and spoon the sauce on top; or add the sauce directly to the pasta, toss gently and serve on warm plates. Tear or snip plenty of parsley over the top, and hand round the Parmesan.

tagliatelle verde with oyster mushrooms & garlic

400g or 14oz tagliatelle verde

salt to taste

25g or 1oz butter

350g or 12oz oyster mushrooms, washed and sliced

1 garlic clove, peeled and crushed

1 quantity of cream sauce (page 13)

freshly ground black pepper

squeeze of lemon juice, optional

1 tablespoon olive oil

sprigs of fresh flat-leaf parsley, to serve

1 Fill a large saucepan with four litres (seven pints) of water and put it on the stove to heat for the pasta.

2 When the water boils, add the pasta along with a teaspoon of salt and stir. Cover until the water has come back to the boil, then let the pasta bubble away, uncovered, for about eight minutes, or until it is tender but still has some bite to it.

3 Meanwhile, cook the oyster mushrooms. Melt the butter in a medium saucepan, add the mushrooms and garlic and cook for four to five minutes, or until the mushrooms are tender and any liquid has disappeared, stirring from time to time.

4 Gently reheat the cream sauce. Add the mushrooms and check the seasoning, adjusting if needed.

5 Drain the pasta by tipping it into a colander placed in the sink, then put it back into the still-warm pan. Either add the olive oil to the pasta, serve it on warm plates and spoon the sauce on top; or add the sauce directly to the pasta, toss gently and serve on warm plates. Chop, snip or tear the parsley over the top.

woodland mushroom & pasta soup

15g or ½oz dried porcini mushrooms

2 tablespoons olive oil

1 onion, peeled and chopped

1 garlic clove, peeled and crushed

450g or 1lb assorted fresh mushrooms,
   including wild ones if available,
   washed and roughly chopped

1 litre or 35fl oz vegetable stock

55g or 2oz small pasta shapes

salt and freshly ground black pepper

2 tablespoons chopped fresh parsley,
   preferably flat-leaf, to serve

1 Put the dried porcini mushrooms into a small bowl and cover with 150ml or 5fl oz boiling water. Leave to soak for fifteen to thirty minutes, then drain, reserving the liquid. Chop the fresh mushrooms.

2 Heat the oil in a large saucepan, put in the onion and garlic, stir briefly, then cover and leave to cook gently for ten minutes, or until the onions start to soften.

3 Add the fresh and soaked mushrooms to the onions. Stir, then cook, uncovered, for fifteen minutes or so until the mushrooms are completely tender.

4 Pour in the stock, then add the reserved mushroom liquid, pouring it through a fine strainer or a piece of muslin to catch any grit (with the packaged porcini now available it is unusual to find any, but best be on the safe side). Bring to the boil, then lower the heat and leave to simmer for five minutes.

5 Put in the pasta and cook for a further six to eight minutes until done. Then season the soup and serve it into warm bowls with parsley scattered on each.

*It's difficult to think anything but pleasant
thoughts while eating a home-grown tomato.*
                                                    Louis Grizzard

4

tomatoey pasta

farfalle in fresh tomato sauce with fresh basil

400g or 14oz farfalle

salt to taste

1 quantity of tomato sauce (page 17),
    made with fresh tomatoes

squeeze of lemon juice, optional

1 tablespoon olive oil, optional

freshly ground black pepper

fresh basil leaves

1 Fill a large saucepan with four litres (seven pints) of water and put it on the stove to heat for the pasta.

2 When the water boils, add the pasta along with a teaspoon of salt and give it a quick stir. Briefly put the lid on until it starts to lift, showing that the water has come back to the boil, then let the pasta bubble away, uncovered, for about eight minutes, or until it is tender but still has some bite to it.

3 Heat the tomato sauce through gently. Check the seasoning, adding a squeeze of lemon juice to taste if it needs it.

4 Drain the pasta by tipping it into a colander placed in the sink, then put it back into the still-warm pan. Either add the olive oil to the pasta, serve it on warm plates and spoon the sauce on top; or add the sauce directly to the pasta, toss gently and serve on warm plates. Grind a little pepper coarsely on top, tear the basil leaves over and serve at once.

farfalle salad with gruyère, cherry tomatoes & spring onions

bunch of spring onions, trimmed and cut
   into long ribbons

400g or 14oz farfalle

salt to taste

3 tablespoons olive oil

1 tablespoon wine vinegar

½ teaspoon Dijon mustard

freshly ground black pepper

225g or 8oz cherry tomatoes, halved

125g or 4oz Gruyère cheese, diced or
   coarsely grated

2 tablespoons freshly chopped or torn
   flat-leaf parsley

1 Fill a large saucepan with four litres (seven pints) of water and put it on the stove to heat for the pasta.

2 Meanwhile, put the spring onion ribbons into icy-cold water and leave on one side to curl.

3 When the water in the saucepan boils, add the pasta along with a teaspoon of salt and give it a quick stir. Briefly put the lid on until it starts to lift, showing that the water has come back to the boil, then let the pasta bubble away, uncovered, for about eight minutes, or until it is tender but still has some bite to it.

4 Make a vinaigrette by putting the oil, vinegar, mustard and a seasoning of salt and pepper into a jar and shaking until thoroughly combined.

5 Drain the pasta by tipping it into a colander placed in the sink, then put it back into the still-warm pan. Drain the spring onions and add them to the pasta along with the tomatoes, Gruyère and parsley. Give the vinaigrette a quick shake, then add to the pasta and stir gently until everything is coated. Serve immediately, or cover and leave until the salad cools to room temperature.

fresh tomato soup with farfalline & basil

2 tablespoons olive oil

1 onion, peeled and chopped

1 garlic clove, peeled and crushed

1kg or 2lb 4oz fresh tomatoes, skinned and
roughly chopped

600ml or 20fl oz vegetable stock

55g or 2oz farfalline or other small pasta shapes

salt and freshly ground black pepper

fresh basil leaves, to serve

1 Heat the oil in a large saucepan, put in the onion and garlic, stir briefly, then cover and leave to cook gently for ten minutes, or until the onions start to soften.

2 Add the tomatoes, stir, then cover and cook for a further ten to fifteen minutes, or until the tomatoes have collapsed.

3 Add the stock, bring to the boil, then lower the heat and leave to simmer for five minutes. Put in the farfalline and cook for a further five to eight minutes.

4 Season the soup to taste, then serve it into warm bowls. Tear some fresh basil leaves over each one.

fusilli lunghi with cherry tomatoes, green peppers & capers

2 tablespoons olive oil

2 green peppers, deseeded and chopped

1 fat, juicy garlic clove, peeled and sliced

350g or 12oz cherry tomatoes, halved

400g or 14oz fusilli lunghi

salt to taste

2 tablespoons capers

2 tablespoons freshly torn flat-leaf parsley

freshly ground black pepper

1 Fill a large saucepan with four litres (seven pints) of water and put it on the stove to heat for the pasta.

2 Meanwhile, heat the oil in a saucepan, put in the peppers and garlic, cover and cook gently for about fifteen minutes, or until the peppers are tender, stirring from time to time. Then add the cherry tomatoes, cover and cook lightly for about five minutes.

3 When the water in the saucepan boils, add the pasta along with a teaspoon of salt and give it a quick stir. Briefly put the lid on until it starts to lift, showing that the water has come back to the boil, then let the pasta bubble away, uncovered, for about eight minutes, or until it is tender but still has some bite.

4 Drain the pasta by tipping it into a colander placed in the sink, then put it back into the still-warm pan and add the green pepper and tomato mixture, the capers, the parsley, and salt and pepper to taste. Toss gently and serve on warm plates.

fusilli salad with cottage cheese, cherry tomatoes & chives

400g or 14oz fusilli

salt to taste

3 tablespoons olive oil

1 tablespoon lemon juice

finely grated or thinly pared rind of ½–1 lemon

½ teaspoon Dijon mustard

1 garlic clove, peeled and crushed

freshly ground black pepper

225g or 8oz cottage cheese

225g or 8oz cherry tomatoes, halved

2 tablespoons freshly chopped chives

1 Fill a large saucepan with four litres (seven pints) of water and put it on the stove to heat for the pasta.

2 When the water boils, add the pasta along with a teaspoon of salt and give it a quick stir. Briefly put the lid on until it starts to lift, showing that the water has come back to the boil, then let the pasta bubble away, uncovered, for about eight minutes, or until it is tender but still has some bite to it.

3 Make a vinaigrette by putting the oil, lemon juice and rind, mustard, garlic and salt and pepper to taste into a jar and shaking until combined.

4 Drain the pasta by tipping it into a colander placed in the sink, then put it back into the still-warm pan. Add the cottage cheese, breaking it up roughly with a fork so that it is in lumps rather than finely distributed, together with the cherry tomatoes and chives. Give the vinaigrette a quick shake, then add to the pasta and stir gently until everything is coated. Serve immediately, or cover and leave until the salad cools to room temperature.

gnocchi, avocado & tomato salad

400g or 14oz gnocchi

salt to taste

3 tablespoons olive oil

1 tablespoon wine vinegar

4 teaspoons Dijon mustard

1 garlic clove, peeled and crushed

freshly ground black pepper

450g or 1lb tomatoes, sliced

2–3 good sprigs of basil, torn or shredded

1 avocado

juice of ½ lemon

1 Fill a large saucepan with four litres (seven pints) of water and put it on the stove to heat for the pasta.

2 When the water boils, add the pasta along with a teaspoon of salt and give it a quick stir. Briefly put the lid on until it starts to lift, showing that the water has come back to the boil, then let the pasta bubble away, uncovered, for about eight minutes, or until it is tender but still has some bite to it.

3 Make a vinaigrette by putting the oil, vinegar, mustard, garlic and salt and pepper into a jar and shaking until combined.

4 Drain the pasta by tipping it into a colander placed in the sink, then put it back into the still-warm pan. Give the vinaigrette a quick shake, then add to the pasta and stir gently until the pasta is coated.

5 Allow to cool, then add the tomatoes and basil. Just before serving, halve the avocado, remove the stone and skin, and slice the flesh. Sprinkle with the lemon juice and salt and pepper and add to the salad. Toss the salad gently, then serve as soon as possible.

lasagnette with spiced lentil & tomato bolognese sauce

400g or 14oz can tomatoes

teaspoon ground cinnamon

1 teaspoon chopped fresh oregano or 1 or 2
teaspoons dried oregano

1 quantity of lentil bolognese sauce (page 18),
made with split orange lentils

salt and freshly ground black pepper

400g or 14oz lasagnette

1 tablespoon olive oil, optional

sprigs of fresh oregano

freshly grated Parmesan cheese, to serve

1 Fill a large saucepan with four litres (seven pints) of water and put it on the stove to heat for the pasta.

2 In the meantime, add the tomatoes, cinnamon and oregano to the bolognese sauce in a pan, breaking up the tomatoes with the spoon. Cook over a fairly gentle heat for ten to fifteen minutes, or until the tomatoes have reduced. Check the seasoning, adding salt and pepper to taste if needed.

3 When the water in the saucepan boils, add the pasta along with a teaspoon of salt and give it a quick stir. Briefly put the lid on until it starts to lift, showing that the water has come back to the boil, then let the pasta bubble away, uncovered, for about eight minutes, or until it is tender but still has some bite.

4 Drain the pasta by tipping it into a colander placed in the sink, then put it back into the still-warm pan. Either add the olive oil to the pasta, serve it on warm plates and spoon the sauce on top; or add the sauce directly to the pasta, toss gently and serve on warm plates. Garnish with fresh oregano and hand round the Parmesan.

lasagnette with sun-dried tomatoes, garlic & basil

400g or 14oz lasagnette

salt to taste

2 garlic cloves, peeled and crushed

1 tablespoon olive oil

4 tablespoons sun-dried tomato purée or
   chopped sun-dried tomatoes

freshly ground black pepper

fresh basil leaves, to serve

flakes of Parmesan cheese, to serve

1 Fill a large saucepan with four litres (seven pints) of water and put it on the stove to heat for the pasta.

2 When the water boils, add the pasta along with a teaspoon of salt and give it a quick stir. Briefly put the lid on until it starts to lift, showing that the water has come back to the boil, then let the pasta bubble away, uncovered, for about eight minutes, or until it is tender but still has some bite to it.

3 Just before the pasta is done, cook the garlic in the olive oil over a gentle heat for two to three minutes, without letting it brown.

4 Drain the pasta by tipping it into a colander placed in the sink, then put it back into the still-warm pan, pour in the garlic and its oil and add the sun-dried tomato purée or chopped sun-dried tomatoes and some pepper. Stir gently, then serve on warm plates. Tear the basil over and scatter the Parmesan on top.

macaroni, cheddar & cherry tomatoes

400g or 14oz macaroni

salt to taste

1 tablespoon olive oil

350g or 12oz cherry tomatoes, halved

175g or 6oz Cheddar cheese,
    coarsely grated or diced

1 Fill a large saucepan with four litres (seven pints) of water and put it on the stove to heat for the pasta.

2 When the water boils, add the pasta along with a teaspoon of salt and give it a quick stir. Briefly put the lid on until it starts to lift, showing that the water has come back to the boil, then let the pasta bubble away, uncovered, for about eight minutes, or until it is tender but still has some bite to it.

3 Drain the pasta by tipping it into a colander placed in the sink, then put it back into the still-warm pan, add the olive oil and toss gently before adding the tomatoes and cheese. Mix again to combine, then serve on warm plates.

macaroni, cheese & tomato bake

225g or 8oz macaroni

salt to taste

teaspoon made mustard

1 egg, separated

175g or 6oz Cheddar cheese grated

1 quantity of béchamel sauce (page 14)

freshly ground black pepper

450g or 1lb fresh tomatoes, sliced

1 Fill a large saucepan with four litres (seven pints) of water and put it on the stove to heat for the pasta.

2 Preheat the oven to 200°C (400°F or gas mark 6). Grease a casserole or roasting tin about 20 x 30cm (8 x 12 inches) and at least 6cm (2½ inches) deep.

3 When the water boils, add the pasta along with ½ teaspoon of salt and give it a quick stir. Cover until the water has come back to the boil, then let the pasta bubble away, uncovered, for about eight minutes, or until it is *al dente*. Drain.

4 Stir the mustard, egg yolk and 55g or 2oz of the cheese into the béchamel sauce in a mixing bowl. Add the drained pasta.

5 Whisk the egg white until it is stiff but not dry, then fold into the macaroni mixture, along with salt and pepper to taste.

6 Pour the mixture into the prepared dish and arrange the tomato slices over the top, placing them very close together. Scatter the cheese over the tomato slices, and bake for about thirty minutes, until the top is golden brown and the inside lightly set.

orzi salad with lemon, olives & fresh herbs

400g or 14oz orzi

salt to taste

3 tablespoons olive oil

1 tablespoon lemon juice

finely grated or thinly pared rind of 1 or 2 lemons

½ teaspoon Dijon mustard

1 garlic clove, peeled and crushed

freshly ground black pepper

55g or 2oz black olives

8 sun-dried tomatoes, chopped

4 tablespoons freshly chopped herbs

1 Fill a large saucepan with four litres (seven pints) of water and put it on the stove to heat for the pasta.

2 When the water boils, add the pasta along with a teaspoon of salt and give it a quick stir. Briefly put the lid on until it starts to lift, showing that the water has come back to the boil, then let the pasta bubble away, uncovered, for about six minutes, or until it is tender but still has some bite to it.

3 Make a vinaigrette by putting the oil, lemon juice and rind, mustard, garlic and a seasoning of salt and pepper into a jar and shaking until combined.

4 Drain the pasta by tipping it into a colander placed in the sink, then put it back into the still-warm pan. Give the vinaigrette a quick shake, then add to the pasta, along with the olives, sun-dried tomatoes and herbs, and stir gently until everything is coated. Serve immediately, or cover and leave until the salad cools to room temperature.

penne arrabbiata

400g or 14oz penne

salt to taste

1 dried red chilli, crumbled

1 tablespoon sun-dried tomato purée

1 quantity of tomato sauce (page 17)

freshly ground black pepper

1 tablespoon olive oil, optional

1 Fill a large saucepan with four litres (seven pints) of water and put it on the stove to heat for the pasta.

2 When the water boils, add the pasta along with a teaspoon of salt and give it a quick stir. Briefly put the lid on until it starts to lift, showing that the water has come back to the boil, then let the pasta bubble away, uncovered, for about eight minutes, or until it is tender but still has some bite to it.

3 Meanwhile, add the red chilli and the sun-dried tomato purée to the tomato sauce in a pan and heat through gently, stirring from time to time. Check the seasoning, adding salt and pepper to taste, if necessary.

4 Drain the pasta by tipping it into a colander placed in the sink, then put it back into the still-warm pan. Either add the olive oil to the pasta, serve it on warm plates and spoon the sauce on top; or add the sauce directly to the pasta, toss gently and serve on warm plates.

penne with chilli
& red beans

400g or 14oz penne

salt to taste

1 dried red chilli, crumbled, or 1 fresh green chilli
    finely sliced

1 x 400g or 14oz can red kidney beans, drained

1 quantity of tomato sauce (page 17)

freshly ground black pepper

squeeze of lemon juice, optional

1 tablespoon olive oil, optional

several good sprigs of fresh coriander, to serve

1 Fill a large saucepan with four litres (seven pints) of water and put it on the stove to heat for the pasta.

2 When the water boils, add the pasta along with a teaspoon of salt and give it a quick stir. Briefly put the lid on until it starts to lift, showing that the water has come back to the boil, then let the pasta bubble away, uncovered, for about eight minutes, or until it is tender but still has some bite to it.

3 Meanwhile, add the chilli and beans to the tomato sauce in a pan and heat through gently, stirring from time to time. Check the seasoning, adding pepper, a squeeze of lemon juice and salt to taste, if it needs it.

4 Drain the pasta by tipping it into a colander placed in the sink, then put it back into the still-warm pan. Either add the olive oil to the pasta, serve it on warm plates and spoon the sauce on top; or add the sauce directly to the pasta, toss gently and serve on warm plates. Chop, snip or tear the coriander over the top.

penne rigate salad with sun-dried tomatoes & artichoke hearts

400g or 14oz penne rigate

salt to taste

3 tablespoons olive oil

1 tablespoon wine vinegar

½ teaspoon Dijon mustard

1 garlic clove, peeled and crushed

freshly ground black pepper

400g or 1 x 14oz can artichoke hearts, drained and sliced

8 sun-dried tomatoes, chopped

125g or 4 oz fresh Parmesan cheese, cut in flakes

4 good sprigs of fresh basil, torn

1 Fill a large saucepan with four litres (seven pints) of water and put it on the stove to heat for the pasta.

2 When the water boils, add the pasta along with a teaspoon of salt and give it a quick stir. Briefly put the lid on until it starts to lift, showing that the water has come back to the boil, then let the pasta bubble away, uncovered, for about eight minutes, or until it is tender but still has some bite to it.

3 Make a vinaigrette by putting the oil, vinegar, mustard, garlic and a seasoning of salt and pepper into a jar and shaking until thoroughly combined.

4 Drain the pasta by tipping it into a colander placed in the sink, then put it back into the still-warm pan. Add the artichoke hearts, sun-dried tomatoes, Parmesan and basil. Give the vinaigrette a quick shake, then add to the pasta and stir gently until everything is coated. Serve immediately, or cover and leave until the salad cools to room temperature.

penne rigate with tomatoes, basil, pine nuts & chilli

2 tablespoons olive oil

900g or 2lb fresh tomatoes, skinned and chopped

2 fat, juicy garlic cloves, peeled and thinly sliced

1 fresh green chilli, deseeded and finely sliced

400g or 14oz penne rigate

salt to taste

25–55g or 1–2oz pine nuts

4 good sprigs of fresh basil leaves, torn

freshly ground black pepper

1 Fill a large saucepan with four litres (seven pints) of water and put it on the stove to heat for the pasta.

2 Meanwhile, heat the olive oil in a saucepan and then put in the tomatoes, garlic and chilli. Cook gently, covered, for ten to fifteen minutes, or until the tomatoes have collapsed.

3 When the water in the saucepan boils, add the pasta along with a teaspoon of salt and give it a quick stir. Briefly put the lid on until it starts to lift, showing that the water has come back to the boil, then let the pasta bubble away, uncovered, for about eight minutes, or until it is tender but still has some bite to it.

4 Drain the pasta by tipping it into a colander placed in the sink, then put it back into the still-warm pan and add the tomato mixture, pine nuts and basil. Toss gently, season with salt and pepper, and serve on warm plates.

pipe rigate with artichoke hearts & sun-dried tomatoes

400g or 14oz pipe rigate

salt to taste

1 x 400g or 14oz can artichoke hearts, drained
   and sliced

8 sun-dried tomatoes, chopped

1 quantity of tomato sauce (page 17)

freshly ground black pepper

squeeze of lemon juice, optional

tablespoon olive oil, optional

fresh basil leaves, to serve

flakes of Parmesan cheese, to serve

1 Fill a large saucepan with four litres (seven pints) of water and put it on the stove to heat for the pasta.

2 When the water boils, add the pasta along with a teaspoon of salt and give it a quick stir. Briefly put the lid on until it starts to lift, showing that the water has come back to the boil, then let the pasta bubble away, uncovered, for about eight minutes, or until it is tender but still has some bite to it.

3 Meanwhile, add the artichoke hearts and the sun-dried tomatoes to the tomato sauce in a pan and heat through gently. Check the seasoning, adding pepper, a squeeze of lemon juice and salt to taste if it needs it.

4 Drain the pasta by tipping it into a colander placed in the sink, then put it back into the still-warm pan. Either add the olive oil to the pasta, serve it on warm plates and spoon the sauce on top; or add the sauce directly to the pasta, toss gently and serve on warm plates. Tear basil leaves over the top, scatter with flakes of Parmesan and serve at once.

ricotta, sweetcorn, basil & parmesan cannelloni

8 sheets of lasagne verde

salt to taste

225g or 8oz ricotta cheese

225g or 8oz can sweetcorn, drained, or
175g or 6oz fresh or frozen sweetcorn kernels

2 tablespoons torn or chopped fresh basil leaves

125g or 4oz freshly grated Parmesan cheese

freshly ground black pepper

2 quantities of tomato sauce (page 17)

1 Cook the lasagne in plenty of boiling, lightly salted water for six to eight minutes, or until tender but still with some bite. Drain and drape the lasagne sheets over the sides of the saucepan and a colander to prevent them from sticking together.

2 Set the oven to 200°C (400°F or gas mark 6). Grease a casserole dish or roasting tin about 20 x 30cm (8 x 12 inches) and at least 6cm (2½ inches) deep.

3 Next, make the filling. Mix together the ricotta, sweetcorn (no need to cook it first), basil and half the Parmesan. Season with salt and pepper.

4 Lay one of the sheets of lasagne out on a board; spoon a line of the filling down the long side of the sheet, then roll it up to enclose the filling and make a cannelloni roll. Cut the roll in half and place in the casserole dish. Repeat using the remaining sheets of lasagne and filling, making two layers.

5 Pour the tomato sauce over the pasta, scatter with the remaining Parmesan and bake for thirty-five to forty minutes, or until golden brown.

spaghetti with ginger-tomato sauce

400g or 14oz spaghetti

salt to taste

a walnut-sized piece of fresh ginger, grated

1 x 400g or 14oz can chickpeas, drained

1 quantity of tomato sauce (page 17)

freshly ground black pepper

squeeze of lemon juice, optional

1 tablespoon olive oil, optional

several good sprigs of fresh coriander

1 Fill a large saucepan with four litres (seven pints) of water and put it on the stove to heat for the pasta.

2 When the water boils, add the spaghetti, holding it straight up like a bunch of flowers and gently pushing it into the water as it softens. Add a teaspoon of salt and give it a quick stir. Briefly put the lid on until it starts to lift, showing that the water has come back to the boil, then let the pasta bubble away, uncovered, for about eight minutes, or until it is tender but still has some bite to it.

3 Stir the ginger and chickpeas into the tomato sauce in a pan, and heat through gently. Just before the pasta is ready, check the seasoning of the sauce, adding pepper, a squeeze of lemon juice and salt to taste if it needs it.

4 Drain the pasta by tipping it into a colander placed in the sink, then put it back into the still-warm pan. Either add the olive oil to the pasta, serve it on warm plates and spoon the sauce on top; or add the sauce directly to the pasta, toss gently and serve on warm plates. Chop, snip or tear the coriander over the top.

spaghetti puttanesca

400g or 14oz spaghetti

salt to taste

1 quantity of tomato sauce (page 17)

2 garlic cloves, peeled and crushed

1 tablespoon sun-dried tomato purée

2 tablespoons capers

55g or 2oz pitted black olives, sliced

1 teaspoon chopped fresh oregano

freshly ground black pepper

1 tablespoon olive oil, optional

1 Fill a large saucepan with four litres (seven pints) of water and put it on the stove to heat for the pasta.

2 When the water boils, add the spaghetti, holding it straight up like a bunch of flowers and gently pushing it into the water as it softens. Add a teaspoon of salt and give it a quick stir. Briefly put the lid on until it starts to lift, showing that the water has come back to the boil, then let the pasta bubble away, uncovered, for about eight minutes, or until it is tender but still has some bite to it.

3 Meanwhile, add the garlic, sun-dried tomato purée, capers, olives and oregano to the tomato sauce in a pan and heat through gently, stirring from time to time. Check the seasoning, adding more – especially pepper – if you think it needs it.

4 Drain the pasta by tipping it into a colander placed in the sink, then put it back into the still-warm pan. Either add the olive oil to the pasta, serve it on warm plates and spoon the sauce on top; or add the sauce directly to the pasta, toss gently and serve on warm plates.

spinach &
ricotta cannelloni

8 sheets of lasagne

salt to taste

25g or 1oz butter

450g or 1lb frozen spinach, thawed,
    or fresh spinach washed

125g or 4oz ricotta cheese

125g or 4oz freshly grated Parmesan cheese

freshly ground black pepper

freshly grated nutmeg

2 x quantity of tomato sauce (page 17)

1 Cook the lasagne in plenty of boiling, lightly salted water for six to eight minutes, or until tender but still with some bite. Drain and drape the sheets over the sides of the saucepan and a colander to prevent them from sticking together.

2 Preheat the oven to 200°C (400°F or gas mark 6). Grease a casserole or roasting tin about 20 x 30cm (8 x 12 inches) and at least 6cm (2½ inches) deep.

3 Next, melt the butter in a large saucepan and put in the spinach. Cook for five to six minutes, or until the spinach is tender, pushing it down into the pan and chopping it with the end of a fish slice or spatula. Drain off any excess water, then add the ricotta, half the Parmesan and salt, pepper and nutmeg.

4 Lay one lasagne sheet out on a board; spoon a line of the filling down the long side, then roll it up to make a cannelloni roll. Cut the roll in half and place in the casserole dish. Repeat with the remaining lasagne and filling, making two layers.

5 Pour the tomato sauce over the cannelloni, scatter with the remaining Parmesan and bake for thirty-five to forty minutes, or until golden brown.

wholewheat fusilli with goats cheese

400g or 14oz wholewheat fusilli

salt to taste

1 tablespoon olive oil or oil from the
  sun-dried tomatoes

8 sun-dried tomatoes, chopped

225g or 8oz goats cheese, diced

freshly torn basil leaves

freshly ground black pepper

1 Fill a large saucepan with four litres (seven pints) of water and put it on the stove to heat for the pasta.

2 When the water boils, add the pasta along with a teaspoon of salt and give it a quick stir. Briefly put the lid on until it starts to lift, showing that the water has come back to the boil, then let the pasta bubble away, uncovered, for about eight minutes, or until it is tender but still has some bite to it.

3 Drain the pasta by tipping it into a colander placed in the sink, then put it back into the still-warm pan, add the olive oil, sun-dried tomatoes, goats cheese and basil, and salt and pepper to taste. Toss gently and serve on warm plates.

*Sex is good, but not as good as
fresh sweetcorn.*

Garrison Keillor

5

veggie pasta

broccoli &
brie lasagne

675g or 1½lb prepared broccoli, cut into
    small pieces

salt and freshly ground black pepper

150–175g or 5½–6oz oven-ready lasagne

1 quantity of béchamel sauce (page 14), or
    2 quantities of tomato sauce (page 17)

200g or 7oz Brie cheese, thinly sliced

1 Preheat the oven to 200°C (400°F or gas mark 6). Grease a casserole dish or roasting tin that measures about 20 x 30cm (8 x 12 inches) and at least 6cm (2½ inches) deep.

2 Cook the broccoli in a little boiling water for four to five minutes, or until it is tender; drain and season with salt and pepper.

3 Rinse the ready–to-use lasagne sheets under the cold tap, then arrange sheets of lasagne in the base of the dish, to cover it. On top of this put first a layer of sauce, then half the broccoli. Top this with another layer of lasagne, then more sauce, a layer of half of the Brie and the rest of the broccoli. Finish with a layer of lasagne followed by the remainder of the sauce and the rest of the Brie.

4 Bake the lasagne for thirty-five to forty minutes, or until the pasta is tender and the top golden brown.

farfalle with goats cheese, thyme & sun-dried tomatoes

400g or 14oz farfalle

salt to taste

2 large carrots, scraped

8 sun-dried tomatoes, chopped

4 good sprigs of thyme, leaves crumbled

1 tablespoon olive oil or oil from the
    sun-dried tomatoes

225g or 8oz goats cheese, diced

freshly ground black pepper

1 Fill a large saucepan with four litres (seven pints) of water and put it on the stove to heat for the pasta.

2 When the water boils, add the pasta along with a teaspoon of salt and give it a quick stir. Briefly put the lid on until it starts to lift, showing that the water has come back to the boil, then let the pasta bubble away, uncovered, for about eight minutes, or until it is tender but still has some bite to it.

3 Meanwhile, heat another, smaller pan with water for the carrots. Grate the carrots, then blanch them for one minute in the pan of water. Drain and return to the pan with the sun-dried tomatoes and thyme. Keep warm.

4 Drain the pasta by tipping it into a colander placed in the sink, then put it back into the still-warm pan, add the olive or sun–dried tomato oil, carrot mixture and goats cheese, with salt and pepper to taste. Toss gently and serve on warm plates.

farfalle with grilled fennel & pine nuts

450g or 1lb fennel bulbs, trimmed, reserving any
    feathery leaves, and sliced into eighths

olive oil

400g or 14oz farfalle

salt to taste

1 quantity of béchamel sauce (page 14)

freshly ground black pepper

squeeze of lemon juice, optional

55g or 2oz pine nuts, toasted

1 Fill a large saucepan with four litres (seven pints) of water and put it on the stove to heat for the pasta.

2 Parboil the fennel in a little boiling water for four to five minutes, or until just tender. Then drain well, brush lightly all over with olive oil, put in a single layer on a grill pan or baking sheet that will fit under your grill, and grill under a high heat until tender and tinged with brown, about four to five minutes. Keep warm.

3 When the water in the saucepan boils, add the pasta and a teaspoon of salt and stir. Cover until the water has come back to the boil, then let the pasta bubble away, uncovered, for about eight minutes, or until it is tender but still has some bite.

4 Gently reheat the béchamel sauce, then chop any reserved fennel leaves and add to the sauce. Check the seasoning and adjust if necessary.

5 Drain the pasta, then put it back into the still-warm pan. Either add one tablespoon of olive oil to the pasta, serve it on warm plates and spoon the sauce on top; or add the sauce directly to the pasta, toss gently and serve on warm plates. Top with slices of grilled fennel and toasted pine nuts and serve at once.

farfalle with mange-tout, lemon & basil

400g or 14oz farfalle

salt to taste

350g or 12oz mange-tout, trimmed

2 tablespoons olive oil

finely grated or thinly pared rind of 1 lemon

juice of 1 lemon

freshly ground black pepper

4 good sprigs of fresh basil leaves

1 Fill a large saucepan with four litres (seven pints) of water and put it on the stove to heat for the pasta.

2 When the water boils, add the pasta along with a teaspoon of salt and give it a quick stir. Briefly put the lid on until it starts to lift, showing that the water has come back to the boil, then let the pasta bubble away, uncovered, for about eight minutes, or until it is tender but still has some bite to it.

3 Just before the pasta is done, add the mange-tout to it and cook briefly, just to heat through.

4 Drain the pasta and mange-tout by tipping them into a colander placed in the sink, then put them back into the still-warm pan, add the olive oil, lemon rind and juice and a grinding of black pepper, and serve on warm plates. Tear the basil over the top.

farfalle salad with asparagus & peas

400g or 14oz farfalle

salt to taste

450g or 1lb asparagus, trimmed and halved

225g or 8oz shelled fresh peas

3 tablespoons olive oil

1 tablespoon wine vinegar

freshly ground black pepper

2 tablespoons freshly chopped or torn mint

1 Fill a large saucepan with four litres (seven pints) of water and put it on the stove to heat for the pasta.

2 When the water boils, add the pasta along with a teaspoon of salt and give it a quick stir. Briefly put the lid on until it starts to lift, showing that the water has come back to the boil, then let the pasta bubble away, uncovered, for about eight minutes, or until it is tender but still has some bite to it.

3 Meanwhile, cook the asparagus in a little boiling water until just tender, about six to eight minutes. A minute before it is done, put in the peas. Drain the asparagus and peas.

4 Make a vinaigrette by putting the oil, vinegar and a seasoning of salt and pepper into a jar and shaking until combined.

5 Drain the pasta by tipping it into a colander placed in the sink, then put it back into the still-warm pan. Add the asparagus, peas and mint. Give the vinaigrette a quick shake, then add to the pasta and stir gently until everything is coated. Serve immediately, or cover and leave until the salad cools to room temperature.

fettuccine with radicchio & pink peppercorns

400g or 14oz fettuccine

salt to taste

olive oil

1 radicchio, finely shredded

freshly ground black pepper

1 tablespoon pink peppercorns, lightly crushed

1 Fill a large saucepan with four litres (seven pints) of water and put it on the stove to heat for the pasta.

2 When the water boils, add the pasta along with a teaspoon of salt and give it a quick stir. Briefly put the lid on until it starts to lift, showing that the water has come back to the boil, then let the pasta bubble away, uncovered, for about eight minutes, or until it is tender but still has some bite to it.

3 Just before the pasta is done, heat two tablespoons of olive oil in a saucepan and stir-fry the radicchio for one to two minutes, or until wilted.

4 Drain the pasta by tipping it into a colander placed in the sink, then put it back into the still-warm pan. Quickly reheat the radicchio, then tip it into the pasta, including the oil, and stir the pasta gently. Add a little extra olive oil if desired, then season with black pepper. Serve the pasta on warm plates and scatter the pink peppercorns on top.

fettuccine southern italian style

400g or 14oz fettuccine

salt to taste

2–4 fat, juicy garlic cloves, peeled and chopped

4 tablespoons olive oil

225g or 8oz rocket, chopped

4 good sprigs of dill, chopped

freshly ground black pepper

freshly chopped parsley or chervil, to serve

freshly grated or flaked pecorino cheese,
    to serve, optional

1 Fill a large saucepan with four litres (seven pints) of water and put it on the stove to heat for the pasta.

2 When the water boils, add the pasta along with a teaspoon of salt and give it a quick stir. Briefly put the lid on until it starts to lift, showing that the water has come back to the boil, then let the pasta bubble away, uncovered, for about eight minutes, or until it is tender but still has some bite to it.

3 Meanwhile, cook the garlic in the olive oil over a gentle heat for two to three minutes, without letting it brown. Keep on one side.

4 Drain the pasta by tipping it into a colander placed in the sink, then put it back into the still-warm pan. Add the garlic and oil, then throw in the rocket and dill, toss gently over the heat so that they warm through briefly, and grind in black pepper to taste. Serve on warm plates, scatter with parsley and chervil and hand round the pecorino, if using.

fusilli & chickpea salad with spring onions

400g or 14oz fusilli

salt to taste

3 tablespoons olive oil

1 tablespoon wine vinegar (red or white)

garlic clove, peeled and crushed

freshly ground black pepper

400g or 14oz can chickpeas, drained

bunch of spring onions, trimmed and chopped

150ml or 5fl oz crème fraîche, optional

1 Fill a large saucepan with four litres (seven pints) of water and put it on the stove to heat for the pasta.

2 When the water boils, add the pasta along with a teaspoon of salt and give it a quick stir. Briefly put the lid on until it starts to lift, showing that the water has come back to the boil, then let the pasta bubble away, uncovered, for about eight minutes, or until it is tender but still has some bite to it.

3 Make a vinaigrette by putting the oil, vinegar, garlic and a seasoning of salt and pepper into a jar and shaking until combined.

4 Drain the pasta by tipping it into a colander placed in the sink, then put it back into the still-warm pan. Add the chickpeas and spring onions. Give the vinaigrette a quick shake, then add to the pasta and stir gently until everything is coated. Serve immediately, or cover and leave until the salad cools to room temperature Either way, offer the crème fraîche separately, if using.

fusilli with chilli, leeks & courgettes

olive oil

225g or 8oz leeks, trimmed, cut into 5mm
    or ¼-inch slices

1 fresh green chilli, deseeded and chopped

225g or 8oz courgettes, trimmed,
    cut into matchsticks

400g or 14oz fusilli

salt and freshly ground black pepper

freshly grated pecorino cheese, to serve

1 Fill a large saucepan with four litres (seven pints) of water and put it on the stove to heat for the pasta.

2 Meanwhile, heat four tablespoons of olive oil in a saucepan and put in the leeks and chilli. Cover and cook gently for six to eight minutes, or until the leeks are beginning to soften, then put in the courgettes and cook for a further three to four minutes, until the courgettes and leeks are tender. Keep the mixture warm.

3 When the water in the saucepan boils, add the pasta along with a teaspoon of salt and give it a quick stir. Briefly put the lid on until it starts to lift, showing that the water has come back to the boil, then let the pasta bubble away, uncovered, for about eight minutes, or until it is tender but still has some bite.

4 Drain the pasta by tipping it into a colander placed in the sink, then put it back into the still-warm pan, add the leek mixture, season with salt and black pepper as necessary and toss gently. Serve on warm plates, and hand round the pecorino.

fusilli lunghi with broccoli, grilled peppers & olives

1 large red pepper or large yellow
   pepper, quartered

400g or 14oz fusilli lunghi

salt to taste

225g or 8oz prepared broccoli, cut in even pieces

1 tablespoon olive oil

55g or 2oz black olives

freshly ground black pepper

fresh basil leaves

flakes of Parmesan cheese, to serve

1 Place the peppers skin-side up on a grill pan. Put under a high heat for ten to fifteen minutes, or until the skin has blistered and blackened in places. Cover the pepper with a plate and leave until cool enough to handle, then remove the skin, stem and seeds, and cut the flesh into strips.

2 Fill a large saucepan with four litres (seven pints) of water and put it on the stove to heat for the pasta.

3 When the water boils, add the pasta along with a teaspoon of salt and stir. Cover until the water has come back to the boil, then let the pasta bubble away, uncovered, for about eight minutes, or until it is tender but still has some bite to it.

4 Meanwhile, cook the broccoli in a little boiling water for about four minutes, or until tender. Drain and keep warm.

5 Drain the pasta by tipping it into a colander placed in the sink, then put it back into the still-warm pan with the olive oil, pepper strips, broccoli, olives and salt and pepper to taste. Stir gently, then serve the pasta on warm plates. Tear the basil over and scatter the Parmesan on top.

fusilli lunghi with spinach, pine nuts & raisins

400g or 14oz fusilli lunghi

salt to taste

2 tablespoons olive oil

450g or 1lb tender spinach leaves, washed

55g or 2oz raisins

freshly ground black pepper

55g or 2oz pine nuts, toasted

1 Fill a large saucepan with four litres (seven pints) of water and put it on the stove to heat for the pasta.

2. When the water boils, add the pasta along with a teaspoon of salt and give it a quick stir. Briefly put the lid on until it starts to lift, showing that the water has come back to the boil, then let the pasta bubble away, uncovered, for about eight minutes, or until it is tender but still has some bite to it.

3 Meanwhile, heat the olive oil in a large pan and put in the spinach. Stir-fry over a high heat for two to three minutes until wilted, then add the raisins and season with salt and pepper.

4 Drain the pasta by tipping it into a colander placed in the sink, then put it back into the still-warm pan, add the spinach mixture and the pine nuts and toss gently. Serve on warm plates.

fusilli & sweetcorn with mixed peppers

400g or 14oz fusilli

salt to taste

225g or 8oz fresh sweetcorn scraped from the
cob or frozen or canned sweetcorn

1 quantity of béchamel sauce (page 14)

1 small red pepper, deseeded, finely chopped

1 small green pepper, deseeded, finely chopped

freshly ground black pepper

squeeze of lemon juice, optional

1 tablespoon olive oil, optional

1 Fill a large saucepan with four litres (seven pints) of water and put it on the stove to heat for the pasta.

2 When the water boils, add the pasta along with a teaspoon of salt and give it a quick stir. Briefly put the lid on until it starts to lift, showing that the water has come back to the boil, then let the pasta bubble away, uncovered, for about eight minutes, or until it is tender but still has some bite to it.

3 Meanwhile, cook the sweetcorn in a little boiling water for three to four minutes, or until it is just tender, then drain and add to the béchamel sauce along with the chopped peppers.

4 Gently reheat the béchamel sauce, then check the seasoning, adding pepper, a squeeze of lemon juice and salt to taste if it needs it.

5 Drain the pasta by tipping it into a colander placed in the sink, then put it back into the still-warm pan. Either add the olive oil to the pasta, serve it on warm plates and spoon the sauce on top; or add the sauce directly to the pasta, toss gently and serve on warm plates.

lumache with feta & broccoli

400g or 14oz lumache

salt to taste

450g or 1lb prepared broccoli,
    cut in 1cm or ½-inch pieces

1 tablespoon olive oil

125g or 4oz feta cheese

freshly ground black pepper

fresh basil leaves, to serve

1 Fill a large saucepan with four litres (seven pints) of water and put it on the stove to heat for the pasta.

2 When the water boils, add the pasta along with a teaspoon of salt and give it a quick stir. Briefly put the lid on until it starts to lift, showing that the water has come back to the boil, then let the pasta bubble away, uncovered, for about eight minutes, or until it is tender but still has some bite to it.

3 Meanwhile, cook the broccoli in a little boiling water for three to four minutes, or until it is just tender, then drain the broccoli and keep it warm.

4 Drain the pasta by tipping it into a colander placed in the sink, then put it back into the still-warm pan with the olive oil, stirring gently so that the olive oil coats the pasta. Then add the feta and broccoli, check the seasoning, toss gently and serve on warm plates. Tear the basil over the top.

noodles with sesame, tofu & spinach

250g or 9oz firm tofu, drained and cut into
   1cm or ½-inch cubes

2 tablespoons dark sesame oil

1 teaspoon grated fresh ginger

2 garlic cloves, crushed

1 tablespoon soy sauce

1 tablespoon tahini

1 tablespoon sesame seeds

1 tablespoon honey or maple syrup

250g or 9oz spinach leaves

salt and freshly ground black pepper

250g or 9oz udon or other noodles

extra soy sauce, to serve

1 Preheat the oven to 220°C (425°F or gas mark 7).

2 Put the tofu into a bowl with one tablespoon of the sesame oil, the ginger, garlic, soy sauce, tahini, sesame seeds and honey or maple syrup and mix gently together.

3 Spread the tofu out on a non-stick or lightly oiled oven tray and bake for about thirty minutes, or until browned and crisp, stirring it once or twice.

4 Cook the spinach in a dry saucepan, pushing it down into the pan over a high heat, until the spinach is wilted and tender – about six to seven minutes. Drain and season with salt and pepper.

5 Bring a large saucepan of water to the boil for the noodles and cook according to packet instructions. Drain, return to the pan and toss with the remaining tablespoon of sesame oil.

6 Divide the noodles and spinach among four plates and top with the crisp tofu. Hand round extra soy sauce separately.

oriental noodle salad

400g or 14oz noodles

2 tablespoons roasted sesame oil

2 tablespoons soy sauce

1 tablespoon rice vinegar (if available)

1 garlic clove, peeled and crushed

125g or 4oz mange-tout, topped, tailed,
    and sliced diagonally

125g or 4oz baby sweetcorn, sliced diagonally

4 spring onions, trimmed and sliced

2 tablespoons chopped fresh coriander

salt and freshly ground black pepper

55g or 2oz roasted peanuts, optional

1 Bring a kettleful of water to the boil. Put the noodles into a large bowl or saucepan, cover generously with boiling water and leave for two to three minutes (or according to the instructions on the packet) until tender, then drain them.

2 Pour the noodles into a serving bowl and add the roasted sesame oil, soy sauce, rice vinegar and garlic. Toss together gently to mix well.

3 Cook the mange-tout and sweetcorn together in a little boiling water for one to two minutes, or until just tender. Drain, refresh under the cold tap and drain again.

4 Add the mange-tout and sweetcorn to the noodles, along with the spring onions, coriander and salt and pepper to taste. Serve immediately, or cover and leave until the salad cools to room temperature. In either case, add the peanuts, if using, just before you serve the salad.

pasta shells with parsley pesto

400g or 14oz conchiglie

salt to taste

a 400g or 14oz can artichoke hearts, drained
and sliced

for the parsley pesto
55g or 2oz fresh parsley leaves

2 garlic cloves, peeled

2 tablespoons pine nuts, toasted

8 tablespoons olive oil

55g or 2oz freshly grated Parmesan

salt and freshly ground black pepper

squeeze of lemon juice, optional

1 Fill a large saucepan with four litres (seven pints) of water and put it on the stove to heat for the pasta.

2 Meanwhile, make the pesto – or this can be done well in advance if you prefer. Follow the recipe on page 16, using parsley instead of basil.

3 When the water in the saucepan boils, add the pasta along with a teaspoon of salt and give it a quick stir. Briefly put the lid on until it starts to lift, showing that the water has come back to the boil, then let the pasta bubble away, uncovered, for about eight minutes, or until it is tender but still has some bite.

4 Scoop up about half a mugful of water from the pasta and set aside. Drain the pasta by tipping it into a colander placed in the sink, then put it back into the still-warm pan. Give the pesto a stir and loosen, if it needs it, by mixing in a couple of tablespoons of the hot pasta water, then add it to the pasta. Toss the pasta gently until it is coated with the pesto, then add the artichoke hearts. Check the seasoning, and serve at once on warm plates.

penne with grilled vegetables

2 courgettes, cut into batons

2 red onions, peeled and cut into eighths

1 aubergine, cut into batons

2 tablespoons olive oil

2 red peppers, deseeded and cut into strips

400g or 14oz penne

salt and freshly ground black pepper

several sprigs of basil, torn

Parmesan or pecorino cheese, grated

1 Turn on the grill to high. Put the courgettes, onions and aubergines onto a grill pan, drizzle with two tablespoons of the oil and turn the vegetables with your hands until they are all coated. Then add the peppers (they cook well without oil).

2 Put under the grill for ten to fifteen minutes, or until the vegetables are tender and blackened in places, giving them a stir halfway through. Keep warm.

3 Meanwhile, bring a large saucepan of water to the boil, put in the pasta and a teaspoon of salt and boil until it's *al dente*, following packet directions.

4 Add the vegetables to the pasta, along with some salt and pepper to taste and the basil, tossing gently to mix. Serve at once and offer the cheese separately.

penne with onions, goats cheese & walnuts

2 tablespoons olive oil

700g or 1lb 9oz onions, peeled, thinly sliced

400g or 14oz penne

salt to taste

125g or 4oz smooth goats cheese, chopped

55g or 2oz shelled walnuts

freshly ground black pepper

1 First, start cooking the onions. Heat the olive oil in a saucepan, put in the onions, stir, then cover and leave over a gentle heat for thirty minutes, until very tender. Stir from time to time, especially towards the end, to make sure they do not stick.

2 Fill a large saucepan with four litres (seven pints) of water and put it on the stove to heat for the pasta.

3 When the water boils, add the pasta along with a teaspoon of salt and give it a quick stir. Briefly put the lid on until it starts to lift, showing that the water has come back to the boil, then let the pasta bubble away, uncovered, for about eight minutes, or until it is tender but still has some bite to it.

4 Drain the pasta by tipping it into a colander placed in the sink, then put it back into the still-warm pan, add the goats cheese and toss gently. Then add the onions and walnuts, and salt and pepper to taste, and serve on warm plates.

penne rigate salad with broccoli & cherry tomatoes

400g or 14oz penne rigate

salt to taste

225g or 8oz broccoli, divided into small florets

3 tablespoons olive oil

1 tablespoon wine vinegar

½ teaspoon Dijon mustard

1 garlic clove, peeled and crushed

freshly ground black pepper

225g or 8oz cherry tomatoes, halved

2–3 good sprigs of basil, freshly torn or shredded

1 Fill a large saucepan with four litres (seven pints) of water and put it on the stove to heat for the pasta.

2 When the water boils, add the pasta along with a teaspoon of salt and give it a quick stir. Briefly put the lid on until it starts to lift, showing that the water has come back to the boil, then let the pasta bubble away, uncovered, for about eight minutes, or until it is tender but still has some bite to it.

3 Meanwhile, cook the broccoli in a little boiling water for three to four minutes until tender. Drain.

4 Make a vinaigrette by putting the oil, vinegar, mustard, garlic and a seasoning of salt and pepper into a jar and shaking until combined.

5 Drain the pasta by tipping it into a colander placed in the sink, then put it back into the still-warm pan. Add the broccoli, cherry tomatoes and basil. Give the vinaigrette a quick shake, then add to the pasta and stir gently until everything is coated. Serve immediately, or cover and leave until the salad cools to room temperature.

penne with rocket, pine nuts & parmesan

400g or 14oz penne

salt to taste

225g or 8oz rocket

2 garlic cloves, peeled, finely sliced or chopped

olive oil

freshly ground black pepper

squeeze of lemon juice

55g or 2oz pine nuts, toasted

55g or 2oz freshly grated or flaked Parmesan cheese

1 Fill a large saucepan with four litres (seven pints) of water and put it on the stove to heat for the pasta.

2 When the water boils, add the pasta along with a teaspoon of salt and give it a quick stir. Briefly put the lid on until it starts to lift, showing that the water has come back to the boil, then let the pasta bubble away, uncovered, for about eight minutes, or until it is tender but still has some bite to it.

3 Just before the pasta is done, stir-fry the rocket with the garlic in two tablespoons of olive oil for two to three minutes, until the rocket is wilted. Season with salt, pepper and a squeeze of lemon juice.

4 Drain the pasta by tipping it into a colander placed in the sink, then put it back into the still-warm pan. Quickly reheat the rocket, then add it to the pasta, along with a little extra olive oil, if you think the mixture needs it, and the pine nuts and Parmesan. Toss gently, check the seasoning, then serve on warm plates.

penne with spinach, mascarpone & parmesan

400g or 14oz penne

salt to taste

125g or 4oz mascarpone cheese, or
  reduced-fat cream cheese

450g or 1lb baby spinach leaves, washed
  and shredded

freshly ground black pepper

fresh Parmesan cheese, cut in flakes or grated,
  to serve

1 Fill a large saucepan with four litres (seven pints) of water and put it on the stove to heat for the pasta.

2 When the water boils, add the pasta along with a teaspoon of salt and give it a quick stir. Briefly put the lid on until it starts to lift, showing that the water has come back to the boil, then let the pasta bubble away, uncovered, for about eight minutes, or until it is tender but still has some bite to it.

3 Drain the pasta by tipping it into a colander placed in the sink, then put it back into the still-warm pan with the mascarpone and stir gently until the cheese has heated through but not boiled.

4 Add the shredded spinach, which will cook in the heat of the pasta, mix gently, season with salt and pepper and serve immediately on warm plates with the Parmesan on top.

penne with vodka & peas

400g or 14oz penne

salt to taste

225g or 8oz podded fresh peas or frozen
    petits pois

1 tablespoon olive oil

2–6 tablespoons vodka, or to taste

freshly ground black pepper

1 Fill a large saucepan with four litres (seven pints) of water and put it on the stove to heat for the pasta.

2 When the water boils, add the pasta along with a teaspoon of salt and give it a quick stir. Briefly put the lid on until it starts to lift, showing that the water has come back to the boil, then let the pasta bubble away, uncovered, for about eight minutes, or until it is tender but still has some bite to it.

3 Just before the pasta is done, add the peas to it and cook briefly, just to heat the peas through.

4 Drain the pasta and peas by tipping them into a colander placed in the sink, then put them back into the still-warm pan, add the olive oil, vodka and a grinding of black pepper, and serve on warm plates.

pennoni with avocado, chilli & coriander

400g or 14oz pennoni

salt to taste

1 garlic clove, peeled and crushed

1 fresh green chilli, deseeded, finely sliced

1 tablespoon olive oil

1 avocado, peeled and sliced

juice of 1 lemon

freshly ground black pepper

4 tablespoons roughly chopped fresh coriander,
to serve

1 Fill a large saucepan with four litres (seven pints) of water and put it on the stove to heat for the pasta.

2 When the water boils, add the pasta, along with a teaspoon of salt, and give it a quick stir. Briefly put the lid on until it starts to lift, showing that the water has come back to the boil, then let the pasta bubble away, uncovered, for about eight minutes, or until it is tender but still has some bite to it.

3 Meanwhile, cook the garlic and chilli in the olive oil over a gentle heat for two to three minutes, until softened but not browned. Keep to one side.

4 Toss the avocado in the lemon juice and season with salt and pepper.

5 Drain the pasta by tipping it into a colander placed in the sink, then put it back into the still-warm pan and add the chilli mixture and avocado. Toss gently and serve on warm plates, with the coriander scattered on top.

pipe rigate with swiss chard, mascarpone & pine nuts

450g or or 1lb Swiss chard, washed

2 tablespoons olive oil

salt and freshly ground black pepper

400g or 14oz pipe rigate

125g or 4oz mascarpone cheese

55g or 2oz pine nuts, toasted

1 Fill a large saucepan with four litres (seven pints) of water and put it on the stove to heat for the pasta.

2 Separate the leafy part of the Swiss chard from the stems. Cut the stems into 1cm or half-inch lengths, then gently cook in the olive oil for about seven minutes until just tender. Add the leafy parts and cook for a further four minutes, or until these are tender, too. Season with salt and pepper.

3 When the water boils, add the pasta, along with teaspoon of salt, and give it a quick stir. Briefly put the lid on until it starts to lift, showing that the water has come back to the boil, then let the pasta bubble away, uncovered, for about eight minutes, or until it is tender but still has some bite to it.

4 Drain the pasta by tipping it into a colander placed in the sink, then put it back into the still-warm pan. Add the Swiss chard, mascarpone and pine nuts, toss gently and serve on warm plates.

red onion & goats cheese lasagne

2 tablespoons olive oil

25g or 1oz butter

700g or 1lb 9oz red onions, peeled and sliced

1 large garlic clove, peeled and crushed

salt and freshly ground black pepper

150–175g or 5½–6oz oven-ready lasagne verde

1 quantity of béchamel sauce (page 14)

200g or 7oz goats cheese log, sliced into
    thin rounds

1 Preheat the oven to 200°C (400°F or gas mark 6). Grease a casserole dish or roasting tin measuring about 20 x 30cm (8 x 12 inches) and at least 6cm (2½ inches) deep.

2 Heat the oil and butter in a large saucepan and fry the onions and garlic gently for thirty minutes, or until they are very tender, stirring from time to time. Season with salt and freshly ground black pepper.

3 Rinse the ready-to-use lasagne sheets under the cold tap, then arrange sheets of lasagne in the base of the dish, to cover it. On top of this put first a layer of béchamel sauce, then half the onions.

4 Top this with another layer of lasagne, then more béchamel sauce, a layer of half of the goats cheese and the rest of the onions. Finish with a layer of lasagne followed by the remainder of the béchamel and the rest of the goats cheese.

5 Bake the lasagne for thirty-five to forty minutes, until the pasta is tender and the top golden brown.

roasted asparagus & fresh herb lasagne

2 bunches of asparagus, tough ends removed,
  the spears cut in half

2 tablespoons olive oil

4 tablespoons chopped fresh herbs: parsley,
  chervil, chives

salt and freshly ground black pepper

150–175g or 5½–6oz oven-ready lasagne

1 quantity of béchamel sauce (page 14)

55g or 2oz freshly grated Parmesan cheese

1 Preheat the oven to 200°C (400°F or gas mark 6). Grease a casserole dish or roasting tin measuring about 20 x 30cm (8 x 12 inches) and at least 6cm (2½ inches) deep.

2 Toss the asparagus in the oil, using your fingers to make sure each piece is coated. Put the asparagus into a shallow roasting tin and roast in the oven for twenty minutes. Then remove from the oven and add the herbs and salt and pepper to taste.

3 Rinse the ready-to-use lasagne sheets under the cold tap, then arrange sheets of lasagne in the base of the dish, to cover it. On top of this put first a layer of béchamel sauce, then half the asparagus followed by a layer of lasagne and more béchamel sauce.

4 Top this with the rest of the asparagus. Finish with a layer of lasagne followed by the remainder of the béchamel sauce and scatter the Parmesan on top.

5 Bake the lasagne for thirty-five to forty minutes, or until the pasta is tender and the top golden brown.

ruote di carro with sweetcorn, peppers & chilli vinaigrette

400g or 14oz ruote di carro

salt to taste

3 tablespoons olive oil

1 tablespoon wine vinegar

½ teaspoon Dijon mustard

1 dried red chilli, crumbled

1 garlic clove, peeled and crushed

freshly ground black pepper

225g or 8oz fresh or frozen sweetcorn

1 red pepper, deseeded and finely chopped

1 green pepper, deseeded and finely chopped

1 Fill a large saucepan with four litres (seven pints) of water and put it on the stove to heat for the pasta.

2 When the water boils, add the pasta along with a teaspoon of salt and give it a quick stir. Briefly put the lid on until it starts to lift, showing that the water has come back to the boil, then let the pasta bubble away, uncovered, for about eight minutes, or until it is tender but still has some bite to it.

3 Make a vinaigrette by putting the oil, vinegar, mustard, chilli, garlic and a seasoning of salt and pepper into a jar and shaking until combined.

4 A couple of minutes before the pasta is ready, add the sweetcorn to the pan – it will only take a minute or two to cook.

5 Drain the pasta and sweetcorn by tipping it into a colander placed in the sink, then put it back into the pan and add the chopped peppers. Give the vinaigrette a quick shake, then add to the pasta and stir gently until everything is coated. Serve immediately, or else cover and leave until the salad cools to room temperature.

spaghetti with béchamel sauce, pesto & parmesan

400g or 14oz spaghetti

salt to taste

1 quantity of béchamel sauce (page 14)

4 tablespoons basil pesto, bought or homemade (see page 16)

freshly ground black pepper

1 tablespoon olive oil optional

55–100g or 2–3½oz fresh Parmesan cheese, cut in flakes or grated

fresh parsley or basil leaves, to serve

1 Fill a large saucepan with four litres (seven pints) of water and put it on the stove to heat for the pasta.

2 When the water boils, add the spaghetti, holding it straight up like a bunch of flowers and gently pushing it into the water as it softens. Add a teaspoon of salt and give it a quick stir. Briefly put the lid on until it starts to lift, showing that the water has come back to the boil, then let the pasta bubble away, uncovered, for about eight minutes, or until it is tender but still has some bite to it.

3 Meanwhile, gently reheat the béchamel sauce. Stir in the pesto and check the seasoning, adding salt and pepper as necessary.

4 Drain the spaghetti by tipping it into a colander placed in the sink, then put it back into the still-warm pan. Either add the olive oil to the pasta, serve it on warm plates and spoon the sauce on top; or add the sauce directly to the pasta, toss gently and serve on warm plates. Scatter generously with the Parmesan and tear or snip the parsley or basil over the top.

sweetcorn, ricotta & cheddar lasagne

450g or 1lb ricotta cheese

300g or 10½oz frozen or canned sweetcorn

125g or 4oz Cheddar cheese, grated

salt and freshly ground black pepper

150–175g or 5½–6oz oven-ready lasagne verde

2 quantities of tomato sauce (page 17)

1 Preheat the oven to 200°C (400°F or gas mark 6). Grease a casserole dish or roasting tin measuring about 20 x 30cm (8 x 12 inches) and at least 6cm (2½ inches) deep.

2 Mix the ricotta with the sweetcorn (no need to cook it) and half the Cheddar. Season with salt and pepper.

3 To assemble the lasagne, rinse the ready-to-use lasagne sheets under the cold tap, then arrange sheets of lasagne in the base of the dish, to cover it. Pour in a little of the tomato sauce.

4 Put in half the sweetcorn mixture, then another layer of lasagne and some more tomato sauce. Follow with the rest of the sweetcorn mixture, the remaining lasagne and the rest of the tomato sauce. Scatter the remaining Cheddar on top.

5 Bake the lasagne for thirty-five to forty minutes, or until the pasta is tender and the top golden brown.

vermicelli
with chickpeas

2 x 400g or 14oz cans chickpeas

400g or 14oz vermicelli

salt to taste

2–4 tablespoons olive oil

2 garlic cloves, peeled and crushed

freshly ground black pepper

1–2 tablespoons chopped fresh parsley, to serve,

2 tablespoons sesame seeds, toasted, to serve

1 Put the chickpeas, together with their liquid, into a saucepan and heat gently.

2 Fill a large saucepan with four litres (seven pints) of water and put it on the stove to heat for the pasta.

3 When the water boils, add the pasta along with a teaspoon of salt and give it a quick stir. Briefly put the lid on until it starts to lift, showing that the water has come back to the boil, then cook the vermicelli, uncovered, for three to four minutes, or until it is tender but still has some bite to it, stirring all the time so that the thin strands do not stick together.

4 Drain the pasta by tipping it into a colander placed in the sink, then put it back into the still-warm pan with two to four tablespoons of olive oil, to your taste, the garlic and a few grindings of pepper.

5 Add the chickpeas to the pasta, toss gently and serve on warmed plates. Sprinkle with the parsley, if using, and the sesame seeds.

vermicelli with spring vegetables

500g or 1lb 2oz vermicelli or thin spaghetti

175g or 6oz baby carrots

175g or 6oz mange-tout

175g or 6oz asparagus tips

2 tablespoons olive oil or butter

2 tablespoons chopped fresh herbs,
   e.g. chives and parsley

salt and freshly ground black pepper

pecorino cheese, in flakes, to serve

1 Bring a large saucepan of water to the boil for the pasta.

2 In the meantime, trim and slice the vegetables as necessary; if they're really baby ones you may not have to do anything except wash them. Cook them in a pan of boiling water, putting in first the carrots then, when they're nearly done, add the asparagus and then the mange-tout, which only need about a minute.

3 When the vegetables are nearly done, put the vermicelli or spaghetti into the pasta pot with a teaspoon of salt and cook until *al dente* – this may only take about three minutes, but be guided by what it says on the packet and what it's like when you bite a bit.

4 Drain the pasta and add the olive oil or butter immediately to stop it sticking together. Drain the vegetables and toss them gently through the pasta along with the fresh herbs and salt and pepper to taste.

Everything you see, I owe to spaghetti.

Sophia Loren